Written by Walch

Illustrated by Jon Lankry

Translated by Ivanka Hahnenberger

Lettered by Frank Cvetkovic

Edited by Justin Eisinger

Collection Edits by Alonzo Simon and David Mariotte

Production by Gilberto Lazcano

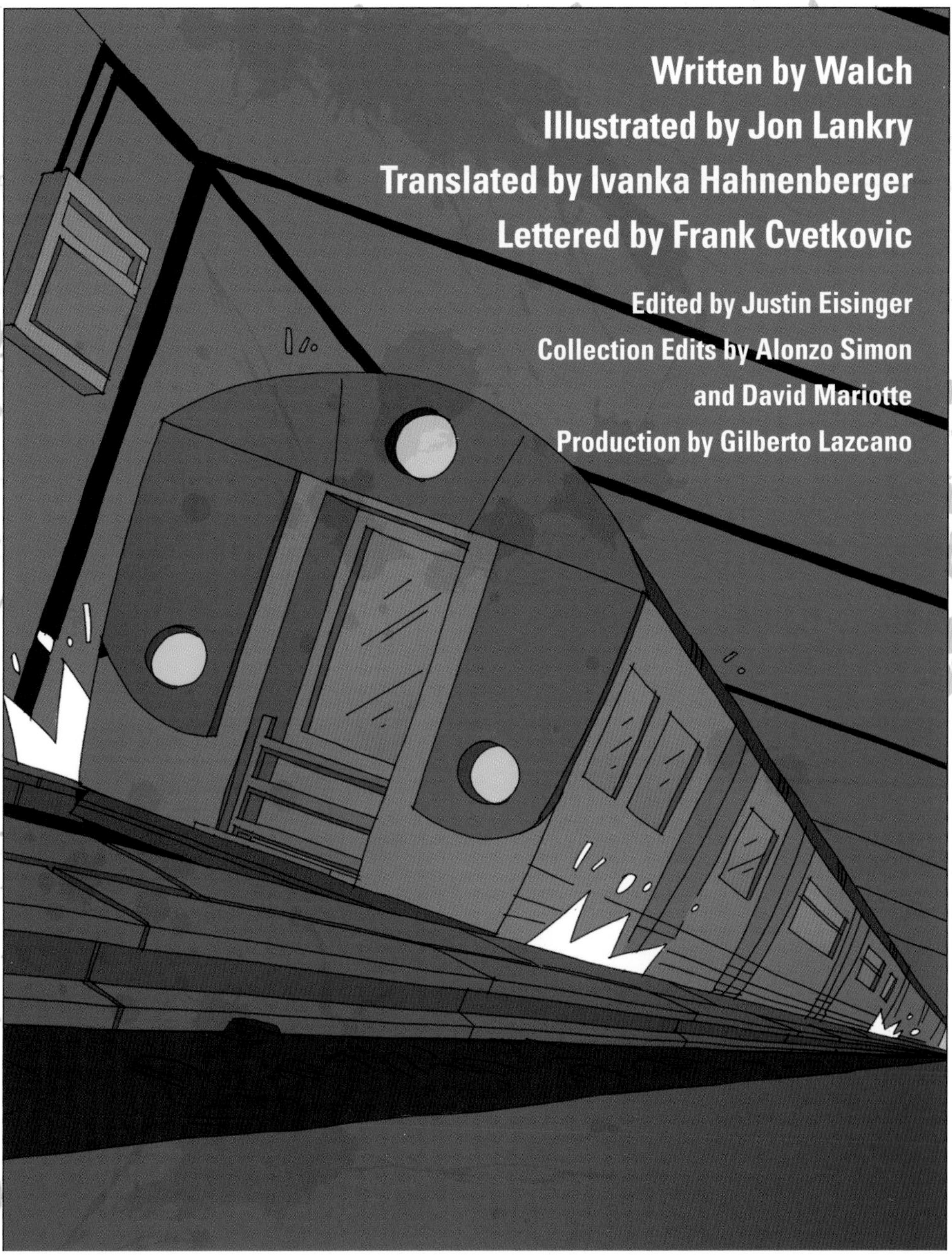

For international rights, contact **licensing@idwpublishing.com**

BN: 978-1-63140-751-2

19 18 17 16 1 2 3 4

DW®

ww.IDWPUBLISHING.com

Ted Adams, CEO & Publisher
Greg Goldstein, President & COO
Robbie Robbins, EVP/Sr. Graphic Artist
Chris Ryall, Chief Creative Officer/Editor-in-Chief
Laurie Windrow, Senior Vice President of Sales & Marketing
Matthew Ruzicka, CPA, Chief Financial Officer
Dirk Wood, VP of Marketing
Lorelei Bunjes, VP of Digital Services
Jeff Webber, VP of Licensing, Digital and Subsidiary Rights
Jerry Bennington, VP of New Product Development

Facebook: **facebook.com/idwpublishing**
Twitter: **@idwpublishing**
YouTube: **youtube.com/idwpublishing**
Tumblr: **tumblr.idwpublishing.com**
Instagram: **instagram.com/idwpublishing**

RAH!
HEY, WATCH OUT!

SCRUNCH
MIOM
SLURCH

HEY!
PAF

SLPR
MÂCH
CROC

HUH?

HEY!!!
GNI HEE HEE

RAAAH
MOM
SCRUNCH

?!
WOW!
HEE
RAAH!
BAM!

HEY!
STOP THAT!

RAH!
HUH?
WHAT THE...?!

RAAH!
SCRIIII
HEE!
AAAH!
THE GUY'S NUTS!

AAAAAAAH!

WHAT... HE... HE'S... EATING HIM!
RAAAH!
SLURK

I... UH...

SCRIIIIIII
RAAAH
OH SHIT!
RAAA
AAAH!

TO CONTINUE THE ADVENTURE YOU NEED TO PICK ONE OF TWO CHARACTERS:

TO PLAY AS BEN, GO TO PANEL 2
TO PLAY AS JUDY, GO TO PANEL 1

RULES OF PLAY FOR JUDY

THE ADVENTURE LOG SHEET IS CRITICAL TO YOUR SURVIVAL. HERE'S HOW TO USE IT:

LIFE POINTS (LP):

YOU START OUT WITH 70 LP. MAKE NOTE OF THAT ON YOUR LOG SHEET.
EVERY TIME YOUR ADVERSARY DOES SOMETHING TO YOU, YOU LOSE LPS.

TO GET THEM BACK YOU NEED TO FIND SURVIVAL OBJECTS SUCH AS:
-DRINKS: 1 LP
-FOOD: 3 LP
-MEDICATION: 5 LP

THESE OBJECTS ARE HIDDEN IN THE PANELS, SO KEEP AN EYE OUT FOR THEM!

THINGS TO KNOW: YOU CANNOT ACCUMULATE MORE THAN 70 LP AT ANY GIVEN TIME.
IF YOU GET TO 0 LP, YOU'RE DEAD AND YOU HAVE TO START ALL OVER AGAIN.

STEALTH POINTS (SP):

THESE POINTS DETERMINE YOUR ABILITY TO BE DISCREET, WHICH IS VERY HELPFUL FOR KEEPING AWAY FROM ZOMBIES! THEY ARE COUNTERED BY VIGILANCE LEVELS. YOU HAVE NO SP TO START WITH BUT DON'T WORRY, YOU'LL QUICKLY FIND OBJECTS THAT CAN PROVIDE YOU WITH THEM... IF YOU'RE VIGILANT!

WEAPONS:

IN ORDER TO SURVIVE YOU'LL NEED TO DEFEND YOURSELF, WHICH MEANS YOU'LL NEED SOME WEAPONS. YOU CAN ONLY CARRY TWO AT A TIME. YOU CAN, AT ANY TIME, GET RID OF ONE TO REPLACE IT WITH ANOTHER.

EACH WEAPON HAS TWO IMPORTANT CHARACTERISTICS:

- *-DAMAGE QUOTA (DQ):* THIS IS THE NUMBER OF LIFE POINTS (LP) YOU TAKE AWAY FROM YOUR ADVERSARY EVERY TIME THE WEAPON I USED AGAINST THEM.
- *-THE AMMUNITION (AM):* SOME WEAPONS HAVE A LIMITED AMOUNT OF AMMUNITION, WHICH IS INDICATED IN THE DESCRIPTION OF THE WEAPON (SEE THE EXAMPLE BELOW). YOU MUST SUBTRACT ONE PIECE OF AMMUNITION EVERY TIME YOU USE THE WEAPON. WHEN YOU RUN OUT OF AMMUNITION YOUR WEAPON IS RENDERED USELESS.

THINGS TO KNOW: YOU START OUT WITHOUT ANY WEAPONS, SO IN THE BEGINNING YOU HAVE TO USE YOUR FISTS. THEY HAVE A DQ OF 1. YOU CAN TAKE THE WEAPONS FROM YOUR ADVERSARIES ONCE YOU'VE DEFEATED THEM... IF THEY HAVE ANY! DON'T SUBTRACT AMMUNITION (AM) FROM AN ADVERSARY'S WEAPON WHEN YOU'RE IN A FIGHT AGAINST IT. THE AMOUNT OF AMMUNITION LISTED UNDER THE WEAPON DETAILS IS HOW MUCH AMMUNITION THERE IS WITH A WEAPON WHEN YOU TAKE POSSESSION OF IT!

EQUIPMENT:

IN THIS SECTION OF THE LOG SHEET, WRITE DOWN THE OBJECTS THAT YOU FIND ALONG THE WAY AND THE EFFECT THEY HAVE ON YOUR CHARACTERISTICS.
BE CAREFUL! YOUR BAG CAN ONLY HOLD A MAXIMUM OF TEN OBJECTS AT A TIME!
-YOU CAN REPLACE ONE OBJECT WITH ANOTHER AT ANY TIME.

THE FIGHTS:

YOU HAVE TO FIGHT YOUR ENEMIES. HERE'S HOW:

-EACH ENEMY HAS CERTAIN CHARACTERISTICS INDICATED ON ITS FACT CHART.
AS JUDY YOU CAN ONLY FIGHT ENEMIES WITH A GREEN FACT CHART.

-FOR EXAMPLE, THIS ZOMBIE HAS 4 LP, A VIGILANCE LEVEL OF 2 AND A WEAPON WITH A DQ OF 2. IF HE STRIKES YOU HE WILL TAKE AWAY 2 OF YOUR LP BECAUSE HIS WEAPON HAS A DQ OF 2. THE VIGILANCE POINTS INDICATE HIS LEVEL OF PERCEPTION. THEY RELATE TO YOUR STEALTH POINTS (SP). IN ORDER TO AVOID FIGHTING YOUR ENEMY, YOU NEED TO HAVE A SP HIGHER THAN HIS VIGILANCE. IN THE EXAMPLE, YOU NEED TO HAVE AT LEAST 3 SP TO AVOID FIGHTING THIS ZOMBIE. OBVIOUSLY, YOU CAN TAKE ON ANY ADVERSARY REGARDLESS OF YOUR SP LEVEL IF YOU'RE FEELING DARING!

FIGHTING:

-THE WEAPONS, THE AMOUNT OF AMMUNITION AND THE DQ NUMBER YOU HAVE WILL DETERMINE HOW MANY TIMES YOU'LL NEED TO USE YOUR WEAPON TO KILL YOUR ENEMY.

THINGS TO KNOW: YOU CAN'T ACCUMULATE DQS ACROSS WEAPONS. YOU CAN ONLY USE ONE WEAPON IN A FIGHT AT A TIME.
ONLY WHEN YOU RUN OUT OF AMMUNITION IN ONE WEAPON CAN YOU SWITCH WEAPONS TO FINISH THE FIGHT.
ONLY AFTER YOUR LAST WEAPON HAS RUN OUT OF POINTS (DQ, AM) CAN YOU USE YOUR FISTS. (1 DQ)

EXAMPLE:
TO KILL AN ENEMY THAT HAS 5 LP YOU CAN: PUNCH HIM (1 DQ) 5 TIMES (1 DQ X 5); IF YOU HAVE A BASEBALL BAT (3 DQ), YOU WOULD ONLY NEED TO STRIKE TWICE (6 DQ).

THE NUMBER OF TIMES YOU NEED TO USE YOUR WEAPON(S) TO VANQUISH YOUR ENEMY IS IMPORTANT AS IT WILL DETERMINE YOUR INJURIES IN THE FIGHT SINCE EVERY TIME YOU USE A WEAPON, YOUR ENEMY USES THEIRS ON YOU IN RETURN AT THE LEVEL OF THEIR WEAPON'S DQ.

AMPLE:
U USE YOUR FISTS AGAINST AN ENEMY WHO HAS 5 LP AND A KNIFE WITH 2 DQ.
U WOULD NEED 5 PUNCHES TO KILL HIM (1 DQ X 5 = 5 DQ).

WILL, HOWEVER, STAB YOU AT LEAST 4 TIMES IN THE FIGHT. THAT IS, EVERY TIME YOU PUNCH HIM HE WILL STAB YOU BACK WITH HIS KNIFE, ST LIKE IN A FIGHT. 5 PUNCHES FROM YOU MEANS AT LEAST 4 KNIFE STABS FROM HIM. THIS MEANS THAT YOU WILL LOSE 8 LP (4 X 2 DQ).

T IF YOU HAVE A WEAPON WITH 2 DQ YOU CAN KILL HIM IN TWO WEAPON ATTACKS WHICH WILL MEAN YOU WILL ONLY GET STABBED ONCE YOU WILL ONLY LOSE 2 LP (1 STAB X 2 DQ)!

NGS TO KNOW: ONCE AN ENEMY HAS BEEN KILLED, THEY ARE DEAD FOR GOOD... HOWEVER, IF YOU END UP ON A PANEL FOR A SECOND IE AND YOU CAN'T REMEMBER IF YOU KILLED THE ENEMY THERE, YOU HAVE TO FIGHT THEM BY DEFAULT!

EAM WORK:

DY CAN SAVE PEOPLE AND AS A RESULT GET ALLIES. HERE'S HOW:

DY HAS A SPECIAL CATEGORY IN HER ADVENTURE LOG (*PAGE 143*) CALLED "GROUP," WHICH MEANS SHE CAN SURROUND HERSELF WITH RTAIN CHARACTERS THAT COULD HELP HER DURING HER ADVENTURE. GROUP MEMBERS ARE CALLED ALLIES WHICH ARE IDENTIFIED BY TTERS (*E.G.: A FOR ANDREA*) AND THEIR PANELS HAVE A FACT SHEET THAT OUTLINE THEIR CHARACTERISTICS.
JUDY, YOU CAN ONLY TAKE INTO CONSIDERATION THE GREEN SECTION ON THE LEFT-HAND SIDE OF THE FACT SHEETS.
E NUMBER OF ALLIES THAT YOU CAN HAVE IS DEPENDENT ON YOUR SP. FOR EXAMPLE, WITH 4 SP, YOU CAN HAVE 4 ALLIES, IF YOU LOSE 1 YOU LOSE AN ALLY!

INGS TO KNOW: THE LETTERS THAT ARE ASSIGNED TO EACH ALLY CORRESPOND TO THE FIRST LETTER OF THEIR FIRST NAME. BE REFUL, SOMETIMES THE LETTERS CAN BE WELL HIDDEN IN THE PANEL ART, YOU NEED TO KEEP YOUR EYES OPEN!

ANDREA, THE NURSE

BONUS POINTS: 3	BONUS POINTS: 3
SKILLS:	LP: 15
FIRST AID.	VIGILANCE: 5
HER MEDICAL KNOWLEDGE ALLOWS YOU TO DOUBLE THE EFFECTS OF SURVIVAL OBJECTS.	WEAPON: SCALPEL (4 DQ, 2 IP)
CHARACTER TRAIT:	HEART: 600 OZ
VOLUNTEER	BRAIN: 400 OZ
C274/I351	MUSCLE: 100 OZ
GO BACK TO 301.	VICTORY -> 320
	FLEE -> 301

ONUS POINTS: EACH ALLY HAS THEIR OWN SET OF BONUS POINTS. THEY HELP YOU CALCULATE YOUR RANKING AT THE END OF THE GAME. HIS MEANS THE MORE ALLIES YOU HAVE, THE HIGHER YOUR RANKING!

KILLS: EACH ALLY HAS THEIR OWN UNIQUE SKILL THAT WILL HELP JUDY ON HER ADVENTURE.

HARACTER TRAIT: EACH ALLY HAS THEIR OWN CHARACTER TRAIT. EACH CHARACTER PANEL WILL HAVE ONE OR MORE LETTERS FOLLOWED Y A NUMBER, FOR EXAMPLE A126. IF YOU HAVE THE ALLY WITH YOU WHO CORRESPONDS WITH THE LETTER, FOR EXAMPLE A, YOU HAVE TO O TO PANEL 126.

HINGS TO KNOW: ONCE YOU HAVE ADDED AN ALLY TO YOUR GROUP, YOU CAN NO LONGER GET RID OF THEM (EXCEPT IN SPECIAL CASES HAT WILL COME UP DURING THE ADVENTURE). SO BE SURE THAT YOU REALLY UNDERSTAND EACH OF THEIR CHARACTERISTICS! YOU CAN USE OUR ALLIES' WEAPONS.

OU CAN FIND ALL THE ALLY FACT SHEETS AT THE END OF THIS BOOK. YOU CAN ALSO DOWNLOAD THEM AT *WPUBLISHING.COM/ZOMBIE-THE-ADVENTURE-IS-YOURS/.*

NE LAST THING: AS JUDY YOU CAN FOLLOW THE GREEN NUMBERS AS WELL AS OTHER NUMBERS ***EXCEPT*** THE RED ONES.

OW THAT YOU KNOW ALL OF THE RULES, YOU CAN START YOUR ADVENTURE: GO TO PANEL 1!

RULES OF PLAY FOR BEN

THE ADVENTURE LOG SHEET IS CRITICAL TO YOUR SURVIVAL. HERE'S HOW TO USE IT:

LIFE POINTS (LP):

YOU START OUT WITH 70 LP. MAKE NOTE OF THAT ON YOUR LOG SHEET.
EVERY TIME YOUR ADVERSARY DOES SOMETHING TO YOU, YOU LOSE LPS. TO GET THEM BACK YOU NEED TO EAT AS MUCH FRESH FLESH AS POSSIBLE... HUMAN PREFERABLY (SEE DETAILS OF "STOMACH" CAPACITY).

THINGS TO KNOW: YOU CAN'T ACCUMULATE MORE THAN 70 LIFE POINTS AT ANY GIVEN TIME.
IF YOU GET TO 0 LP YOU'RE "DEAD" AND YOU HAVE TO START ALL OVER AGAIN.

INTELLIGENCE POINTS (IP):

THESE POINTS WILL HELP WITH TWO THINGS:
-*CHOOSING THE RIGHT WEAPON AND SOLVING RIDDLES.* A ZOMBIE NEEDS SOME INTELLIGENCE TO USE A GUN!
-*AVOID FIGHTS.* USUALLY ENEMIES RECOGNIZE ZOMBIES STRAIGHT AWAY FROM THE WAY THEY ACT. SO A HIGH INTELLECTUAL ABILITY WILL HELP TO PASS UNNOTICED!

YOU HAVE NO IP TO START WITH BUT DON'T WORRY, YOU'LL QUICKLY FIND OBJECTS THAT CAN PROVIDE YOU WITH SOME...IF YOU'RE VIGILANT!

WEAPONS:

IN ORDER TO SURVIVE YOU'LL NEED TO DEFEND YOURSELF WHICH MEANS YOU'LL NEED SOME WEAPONS. YOU CAN ONLY CARRY TWO AT A TIME. YOU CAN, AT ANY TIME, GET RID OF ONE TO REPLACE IT WITH ANOTHER.

EACH WEAPON HAS THREE IMPORTANT CHARACTERISTICS:

- -*DAMAGE QUOTA (DQ):* THIS IS THE NUMBER OF LIFE POINTS (LP) THAT THE WEAPON TAKES AWAY FROM YOUR ADVERSARY EVERY TIME IT IS USED AGAINST THEM.
- -*THE AMMUNITION (AM):* CERTAIN WEAPONS HAVE A LIMITED AMOUNT OF AMMUNITION WHICH IS INDICATED IN THE DESCRIPTION OF THE WEAPON (*SEE THE EXAMPLE BELOW*). YOU MUST SUBTRACT ONE PIECE OF AMMUNITION EVERY TIME YOU USE THE WEAPON. WHEN YOU RUN OUT OF AMMUNITION YOUR WEAPON IS RENDERED USELESS.
- -*INTELLIGENCE POINTS IP:* THE MINIMUM NUMBER OF IP NEEDED TO USE THE WEAPON.

THINGS TO KNOW: YOU START OUT WITHOUT ANY WEAPONS SO IN THE BEGINNING YOU HAVE TO USE YOUR FISTS. THEY HAVE 1 DQ! YOU CAN TAKE THE WEAPONS FROM YOUR ADVERSARIES ONCE YOU'VE DEFEATED THEM... IF THEY HAVE ANY! DON'T SUBTRACT AMMUNITION (AM) FROM AN ADVERSARY'S WEAPON WHEN YOU'RE IN A FIGHT AGAINST IT. THE AMOUNT OF AMMUNITION LISTED UNDER THE WEAPON DETAILS IS HOW MUCH AMMUNITION THERE IS WITH A WEAPON WHEN YOU TAKE POSSESSION OF IT!

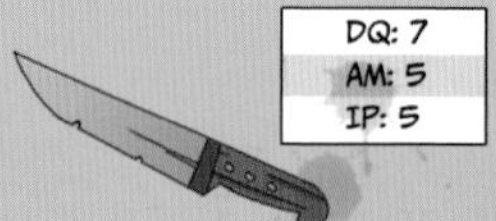

EQUIPMENT:

IN THIS SECTION OF THE LOG SHEET WRITE DOWN THE OBJECTS THAT YOU FIND ALONG THE WAY AND THE EFFECT THEY HAVE ON YOUR CHARACTERISTICS.
BE CAREFUL! YOUR BAG CAN ONLY HOLD A MAXIMUM OF TEN OBJECTS AT A TIME!
YOU CAN REPLACE ONE OBJECT WITH ANOTHER AT ANY TIME.

THE FIGHTS:

YOU HAVE TO FIGHT YOUR ENEMIES. HERE'S HOW:

-WHEN YOU COME ACROSS AN ENEMY YOUR ZOMBIE INSTINCTS WILL FORCE YOU TO FIGHT! EACH ENEMY HAS A FACT SHEET. AS BEN YOU CAN ONLY FIGHT THE ENEMIES THAT HAVE A RED FACT SHEET.

-FOR EXAMPLE, THIS SURVIVOR HAS 4 LP, A VIGILANCE LEVEL OF 2 AND A WEAPON WITH A DQ OF 2. IF HE STRIKES YOU, HE WILL TAKE AWAY 2 LP BECAUSE HIS WEAPON HAS A DQ OF 2. THE VIGILANCE POINTS INDICATE HIS ATTENTION LEVEL. TO AVOID FIGHTING THE ENEMY YOU NEED TO HAVE AN IP HIGHER THAN HIS VIGILANCE. IN THE EXAMPLE HERE YOU WOULD NEED TO HAVE AT LEAST 3 IP TO AVOID FIGHTING THIS ENEMY. OBVIOUSLY, EVEN IF YOU HAVE THE POINTS, YOU CAN TAKE HIM ON ANYWAY IF YOU'RE FEELING BELLIGERENT!

-THE BODY PARTS THAT YOU'RE ALLOWED TO EAT ONCE YOU HAVE DEFEATED YOUR ENEMY ARE: THE HEART, BRAIN AND MUSCLES (*SEE "STOMACH" CONTENTS CHART ON THE OPPOSITE PAGE*).

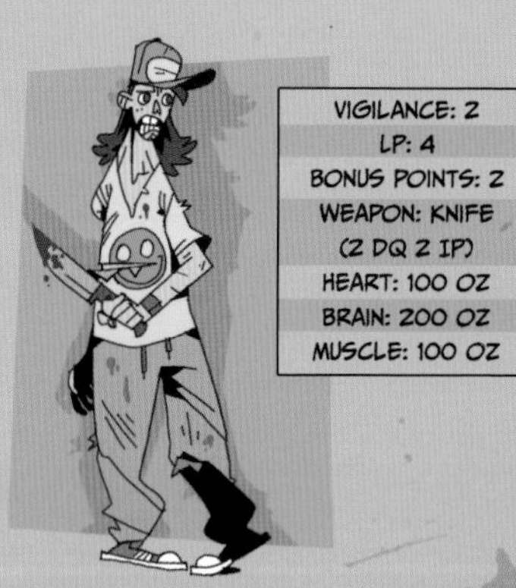

BONUS POINTS: EACH ENEMY HAS THEIR OWN SET OF BONUS POINTS. THEY HELP YOU CALCULATE YOUR RANKING AT THE END OF THE ADVENTURE. THAT MEANS THE MORE OF YOUR ENEMIES THAT YOU EAT, THE HIGHER YOUR RANKING IN THE END!

THE FIGHTS HAPPEN IN THE FOLLOWING MANNER:

-THE WEAPONS AND THE DQ LEVEL WILL DETERMINE THE NUMBER OF TIMES YOU'LL NEED TO USE YOUR WEAPON TO KILL YOUR ENEMY.

THINGS TO KNOW: YOU CAN'T ACCUMULATE DQ ACROSS WEAPONS.
YOU CAN ONLY USE ONE WEAPON AT A TIME IN A FIGHT.
ONLY WHEN YOU RUN OUT OF AMMUNITION IN ONE WEAPON CAN YOU USE THE OTHER ONE TO FINISH THE FIGHT.
IF YOU RUN OUT OF AMMUNITION IN THE SECOND WEAPON, YOU CAN THEN USE YOUR FISTS (1 DQ)

XAMPLE:
) KILL AN ENEMY THAT HAS 5 LP, YOU HAVE TO PUNCH HIM 5 TIMES USING 1 DQ EACH TIME (5 DQ); IF YOU HAVE A BASEBALL BAT (3 DQ), OU'LL ONLY NEED TO HIT HIM WITH IT TWICE (6 DQ).

HE NUMBER OF TIMES YOU NEED TO USE YOUR WEAPON(S) TO VANQUISH YOUR ENEMY IS IMPORTANT AS IT WILL DETERMINE YOUR INJURIES THE FIGHT, SINCE EVERY TIME YOU USE A WEAPON, YOUR ENEMY USES THEIRS ON YOU IN RETURN AT THE LEVEL OF THEIR WEAPON'S DQ.

XAMPLE:
OU ATTACK AN ENEMY THAT HAS 5 LP ARMED WITH A KNIFE WITH 2 DQ.
OU WILL KILL HIM WITH 5 PUNCHES AT 1 DQ EACH = 5 DQ.

E WILL, HOWEVER, STAB YOU AT LEAST 4 TIMES IN THE FIGHT. THAT IS, EVERY TIME YOU PUNCH HIM HE WILL STAB YOU BACK WITH HIS KNIFE, JST LIKE IN A FIGHT. 5 PUNCHES FROM YOU MEANS AT LEAST 4 KNIFE STABS FROM HIM. THIS MEANS THAT YOU WILL LOSE 8 LP (4 X 2 DQ).

JT IF YOU HAVE A WEAPON WITH 2 DQ YOU CAN KILL HIM IN TWO WEAPON ASSAULTS WHICH WILL MEAN YOU WILL ONLY GET STABBED ONCE) YOU WILL ONLY LOSE 2 LP (1 STAB X 2 DQ)!

HINGS TO KNOW: ONCE AN ENEMY HAS BEEN KILLED, THEY ARE DEAD FOR GOOD... HOWEVER, IF YOU END UP ON A PANEL FOR A SECOND ME AND YOU CAN'T REMEMBER IF YOU KILLED THE ENEMY LAST TIME YOU WERE THERE, YOU HAVE TO FIGHT THEM BY DEFAULT!

TOMACH CAPACITY:

EN CAN EAT THE ENEMIES HE HAS VANQUISHED AS WELL AS ANY OTHER BODIES. HERE'S HOW:
EN HAS A SPECIAL CATEGORY IN HIS ADVENTURE LOG (*PAGE 144*) CALLED "STOMACH." AFTER EATING THE ALLOWED ENEMY BODY PARTS HEART, BRAIN OR MUSCLE) THEY ARE STORED AS POUNDS OF FLESH IN THE STOMACH. THE AMOUNT OF FLESH CAN ACCUMULATE.

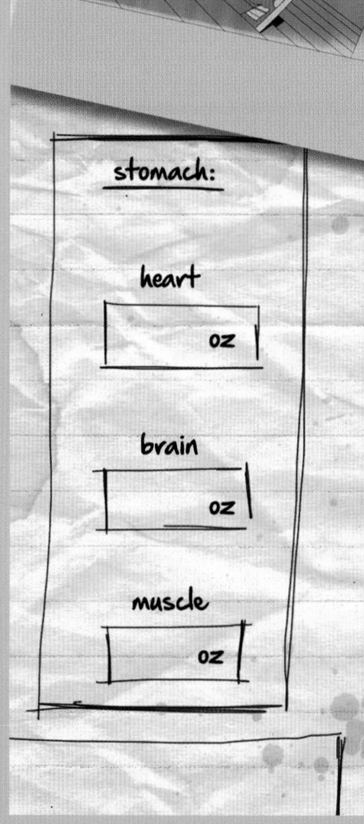

OU CAN CHOOSE TO DIGEST A PART OF WHAT YOU HAVE STORED (*SUBTRACT IT FROM YOUR JOURNAL*) WHICH WILL GIVE YOU THE OLLOWING:

HE HEART: DIGEST 100 OZ AND YOU GET 1 LP
HE BRAIN: DIGEST 200 OZ AND YOU CAN PERMANENTLY INCREASE YOUR IP BY 1
HE MUSCLE: DIGEST 100 OZ AND YOUR WEAPONS' DQ IS INCREASED BY 2.

OU CAN DOWNLOAD, PRINT AND CUT OUT ALL OF THE CHARACTER FACT SHEETS AT ***IDWPUBLISHING.COM/ZOMBIE-THE-ADVENTURE-IS-OURS/***. YOU ALSO HAVE A COPY AT THE END OF THE BOOK.

NE LAST THING: AS BEN YOU CAN FOLLOW THE RED NUMBERS AS WELL AS OTHER NUMBERS ***EXCEPT*** THE GREEN ONES.

OW THAT YOU KNOW ALL OF THE RULES, YOU CAN START YOUR ADVENTURE: GO TO PANEL 2!

1

YOU HAVE CHOSEN TO CONTINUE YOUR ADVENTURE AS JUDY. YOUR GOAL IS SIMPLE:
ESCAPE FROM THIS TOWN WHICH HAS BEEN INVADED BY ZOMBIES!
YOU CAN SAVE OTHER PEOPLE ALONG THE WAY, BUT REMEMBER THE FUNDAMENTAL RULE:
YOU MUST SURVIVE!
NOW CUT OUT THE GREEN ADVENTURE JOURNAL AT THE END OF THIS BOOK
(OR DOWNLOAD AND PRINT ONE FROM IDWPUBLISHING.COM/ZOMBIE-THE-ADVENTURE-IS-YOURS/).
READ THE RULES ON PAGES 6 AND 7. IF YOU ALREADY HAVE, GO TO PANEL 3.

2

YOU HAVE CHOSEN TO CONTINUE YOUR ADVENTURE AS BEN. YOUR GOAL IS SIMPLE:
TO GET OUT OF TOWN BEFORE THE ARMY GETS THERE!
OBVIOUSLY YOU CAN EAT ANY FLESH YOU COME ACROSS ALONG THE WAY...
NOW CUT OUT THE RED ADVENTURE JOURNAL AT THE END OF THIS BOOK
(OR DOWNLOAD AND PRINT ONE FROM IDWPUBLISHING.COM/ZOMBIE-THE-ADVENTURE-IS-YOURS/).
READ THE RULES ON PAGES 8 AND 9. IF YOU ALREADY HAVE, GO TO PANEL 3.

3

BAR BRASSERIE
PHAR
TELEPHONE
TELEPHONE
360
118
SP : 0
-> 137
321
200
233
67
YOU NEED TO GET OUT OF THE CENTER OF TOWN AS QUICKLY AS POSSIBLE.
IT IS YOUR ONLY CHANCE TO SURVIVE! A QUICK GLANCE AT THE MAP IN PANEL 200 MIGHT HELP!

4

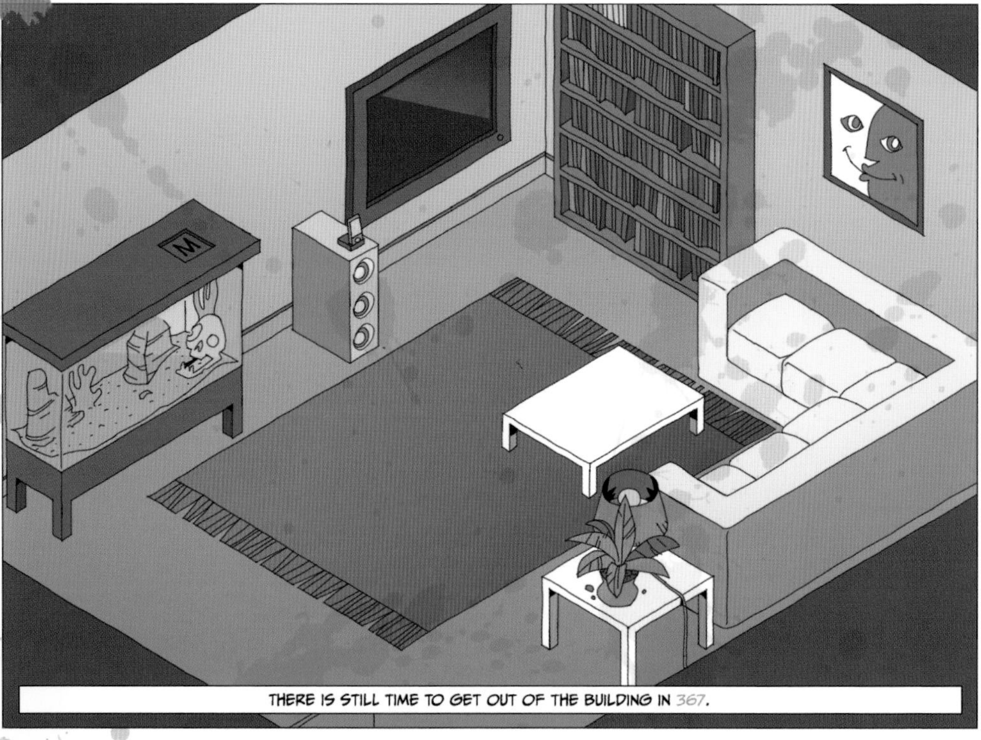

THERE IS STILL TIME TO GET OUT OF THE BUILDING IN 367.

5

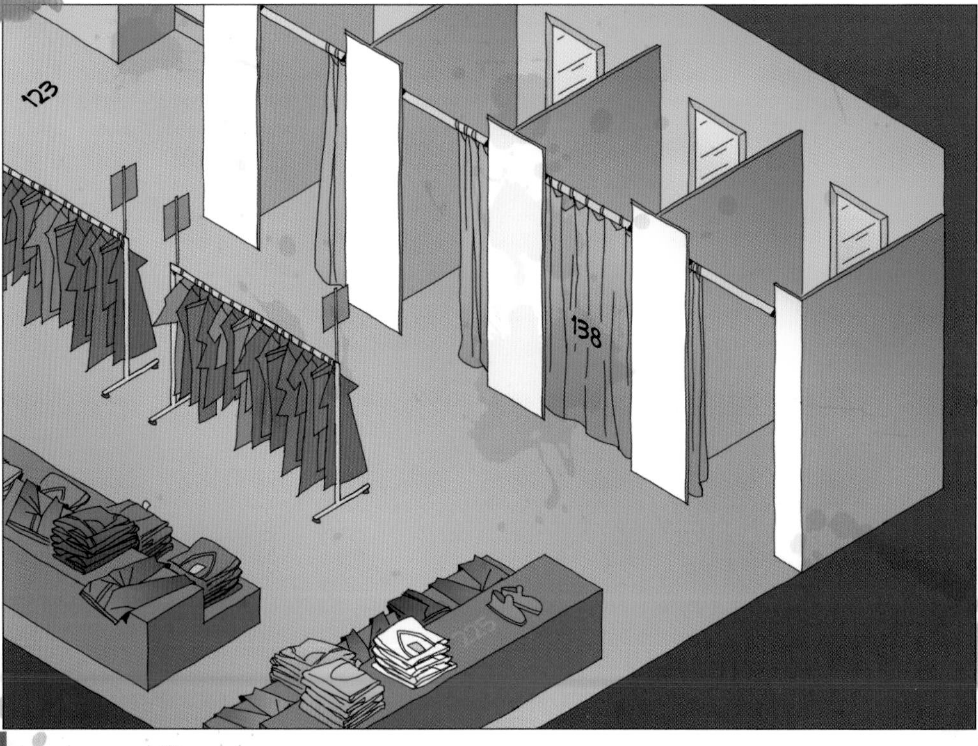

123

138

225

6

MINIPROX SUPERMARKET GENERAL FOOD STORE

170

LP: 14
VIGILANCE: 1
BITE: 3 DQ
VICTORY -> 121

YOU CAN HELP YOUR FELLOW ZOMBIE OPEN THE GRILL IN 115.

7

PUBLIC POOL

205

LP: 6
VIGILANCE: 2
SHARPENED FAKE NAILS: 2 DQ

196

359

IF YOU HAVE ALREADY BEEN IN THE POOL DURING YOUR ADVENTURE YOU CAN NO LONGER GO TO 196.

8

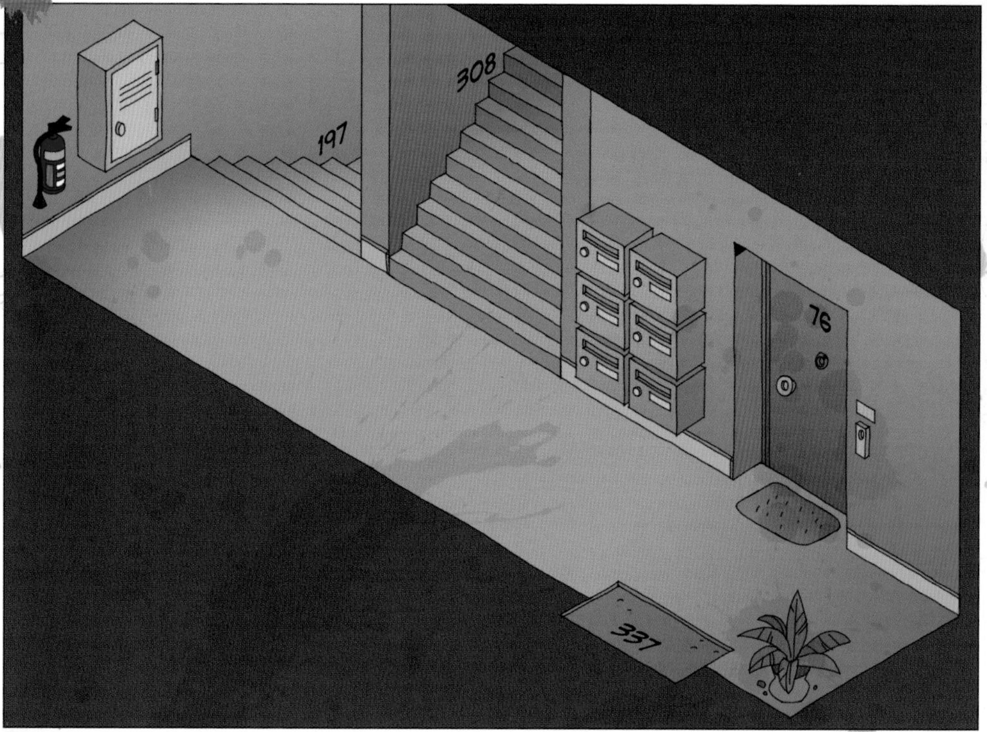

308
197
76
337

9

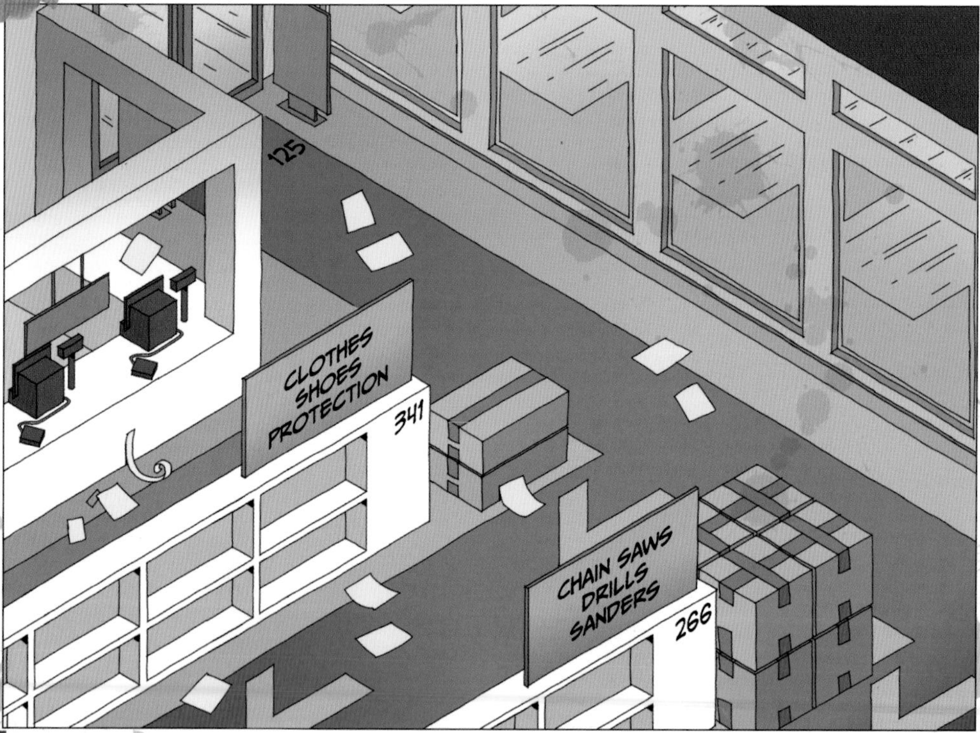

125
CLOTHES
SHOES
PROTECTION
341
CHAIN SAWS
DRILLS
SANDERS
266

10

11

12

13

W14

15

16

270
369

17

AND OBVIOUSLY NO KEY IN THE IGNITION.
YOU MANAGE TO ESCAPE TO 158
WITHOUT GETTING HURT.

18

180
LP: 8
VIGILANCE: 3
WEAPON: SCALPEL (4 DQ)
25
116

19

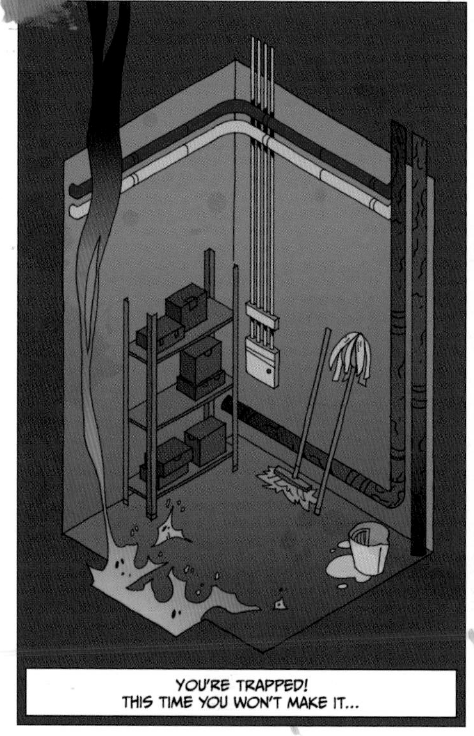

YOU'RE TRAPPED!
THIS TIME YOU WON'T MAKE IT...

20

248
156
94
IF YOU'VE ALREADY BEEN IN THE FAST FOOD RESTAURANT IN THIS ADVENTURE, YOU CAN NO LONGER GO TO 156.

21

THIS ZOMBIE THINKS YOU ARE ONE OF THE LIVING! FIGHT HIM LIKE AN ENEMY.
SURPRISE ATTACK: THE ENEMY STRIKES FIRST.
LP: 8
VIGILANCE: 4
STICK: 3 DQ
159
316

22

334
HEART : 300 OZ
BRAIN: 200 OZ
MUSCLE: 100 OZ
151

23

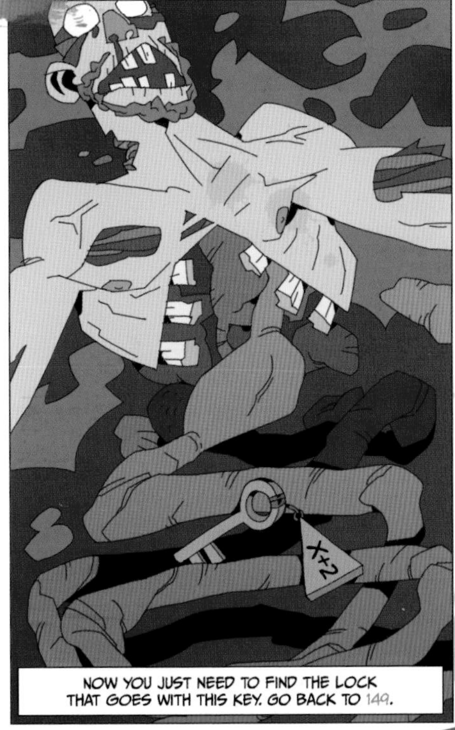
NOW YOU JUST NEED TO FIND THE LOCK THAT GOES WITH THIS KEY. GO BACK TO 149.

24

236

174

205

25

THERE ARE 28 LETTERED PANELS

P@NEL

18

26

LP: 8
VIGILANCE: 6
WEAPON: BROOMSTICK (2 DQ, 2 IP)
HEART: 300 OZ
BRAIN: 300 OZ
MUSCLE: 100 OZ
213

27

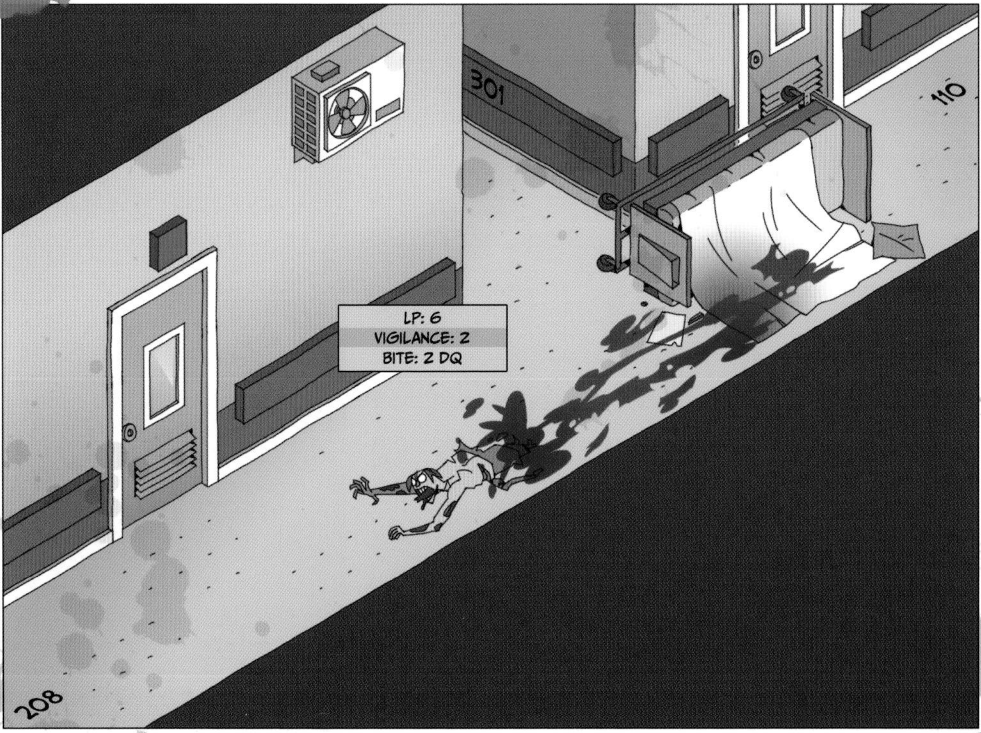

301
110
LP: 6
VIGILANCE: 2
BITE: 2 DQ
208

RAAAH!
POW

STUMP
RAAA
RAAAH

SCRUNCH
SLRP
SLURCH
SLURK

BLAM
BLAM

RAAA

RAAH
RAAA

RAAAH!
NOW YOU ARE A ZOMBIE!
GO TO 2.

29

30

31

LP: 10
VIGILANCE: 4
BITE: 2 DQ
VICTORY -> 183

DENISE DOESN'T GET AWAY. REMOVE HER FROM YOUR GROUP IF SHE'S IN IT.

32

33

GO BACK TO PAGE 2

34

READING THIS BOOK GIVES YOU 2 SP (JUDY) OR 2 IP (BEN). GO BACK TO 198.

T35

YOU CAN EITHER TAKE THE OLD GRUMP (T) OR THE PRETTY WAITRESS (X). ONCE YOU'VE MADE YOUR DECISION GO TO 282 (UNLESS YOU CAN GO TO K97 OR W382).

36

IF YOU RUB YOUR BODY ON THESE ZOMBIE REMAINS, YOU CAN HIDE YOUR SMELL AND GAIN 1 SP. GO BACK TO 20.

37

YOU HAVE TO AIM FOR THE HEAD, EVEN KIDS KNOW THAT... (+1 SP) THIS REMINDS YOU OF SOMETHING. (+1 IP)

GO BACK TO 102.

38

YOU NEED TO ELBOW YOUR WAY THROUGH TO 324... YOU LOSE 3 LP DOING IT.

39

TAKE THIS AS A THANK YOU PRESENT. IT OPENS THE FRONT DOOR OF MY STORE. YOU'LL FIND SOME THINGS TO HELP YOUR CHANCES OF SURVIVAL! GO TO 303 THEN HEAD SOUTHWEST.
TAKE ZOE OUT OF YOUR GROUP BUT KEEP THE BONUS POINTS.

40

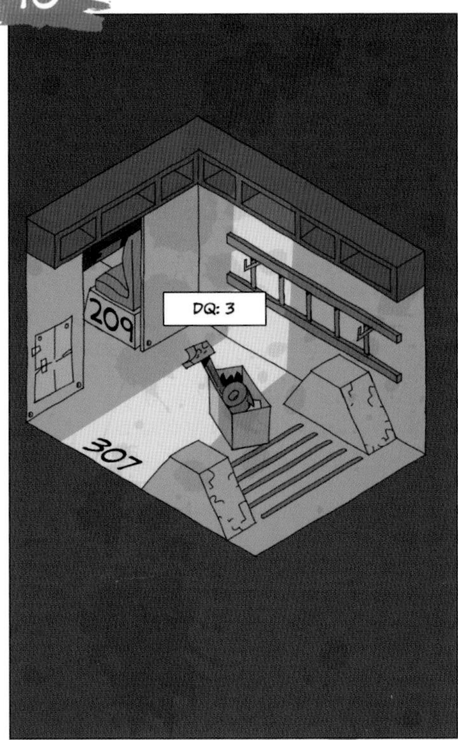
209
DQ: 3
307

41

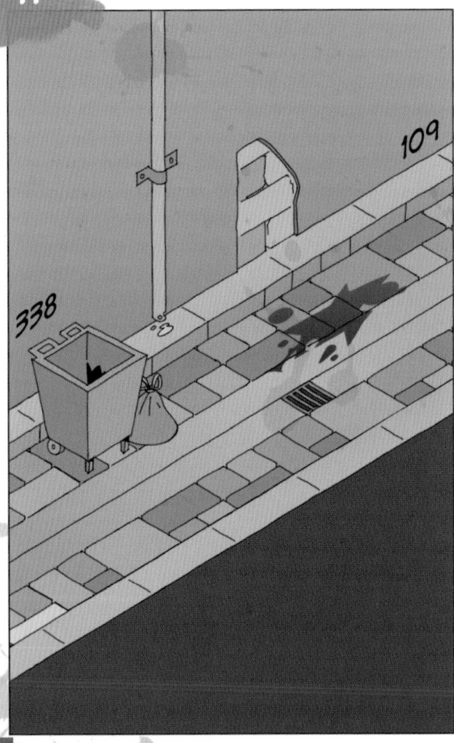
109
338

42

DQ: 7
IP: 5
GO BACK TO 300.

43

IMPROVE YOUR CONCENTRATION WITH QUICKBRAIN!
VITAMINS FOR YOUR BRAIN!
THIS AD IS RIGHT, THESE PILLS WILL GIVE YOU 2 SP OR 1 IP. TAKE NOTE AND GO BACK TO 211.

44
305
261
LP: 6
VIGILANCE: 6
WEAPON: CLAWS (2 DQ)
HEART: 200 OZ
BRAIN: 100 OZ
MUSCLE: 300 OZ
VICTORY-> 128
265

45

LP: 10
VIGILANCE: 10
WEAPON: BASEBALL BAT (5 DQ, 3 IP)
VICTORY-> 135
LP: 5
VIGILANCE: 10
WEAPON: GUN (7 DQ, 2 AM, 5 IP)
VICTORY-> 135
FIGHT ONE OF THE TWO TO GET AWAY, IT'S UP TO YOU TO DECIDE WHICH ONE!

N46

POLICE! PUT DOWN YO...
THROW NORBERT OUT OF YOUR GROUP... YOU CAN GET YOUR REVENGE FOR HIM BY GOING TO E OR YOU CAN RUN AWAY TO 54.

47

A48

49

50

51

52

53

116

GET OUT OF THERE FAST OR YOU'LL BE BBQ'D!
MAKE A NOTE THAT YOU CAN NEVER GO BACK TO THE HOSPITAL BECAUSE OF THE FIRE.

206

149

55

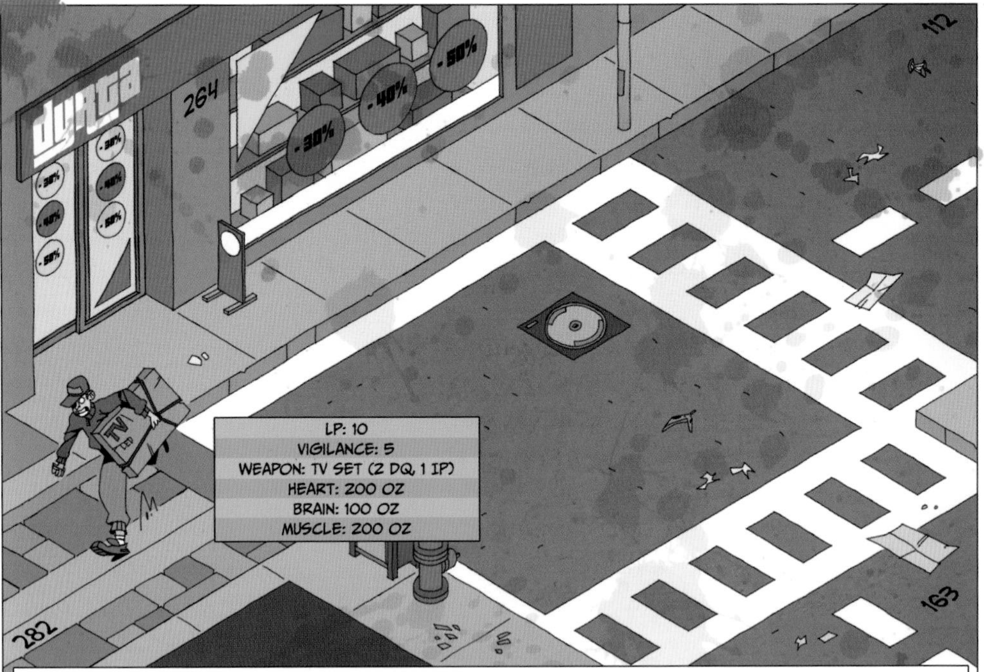

264

112

LP: 10
VIGILANCE: 5
WEAPON: TV SET (2 DQ, 1 IP)
HEART: 200 OZ
BRAIN: 100 OZ
MUSCLE: 200 OZ

163

282

IF YOU HAVE ALREADY BEEN IN THE ELECTRONICS STORE ON YOUR ADVENTURE, YOU CAN NO LONGER GO TO 264.

56

HEART: 300 OZ
BRAIN: 200 OZ
MUSCLE: 100 OZ

160

YOU CAN LEAVE THE POLICE STATION THROUGH 104.

57

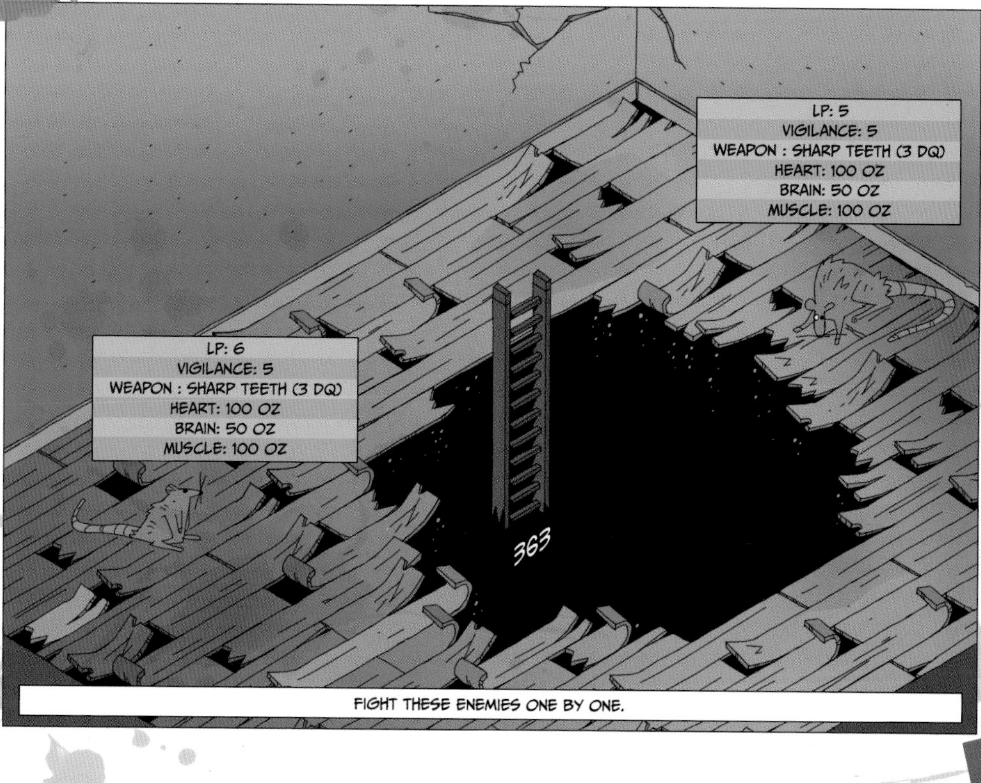

58

FIGHT THESE ENEMIES ONE BY ONE.

59

LP: 8
VIGILANCE: 1
BITE : 3 DQ

204

60

364

252

YOU CAN ALSO GO BACK TO 120.

61

IF YOU HAVE 4 SP OR MORE, YOU CAN TRY AND PASS AS ONE OF THEM BY STOMPING AND ROARING. SEE YOU AT 222. OTHERWISE, EXIT THE THEATRE QUIETLY THROUGH 217.

62

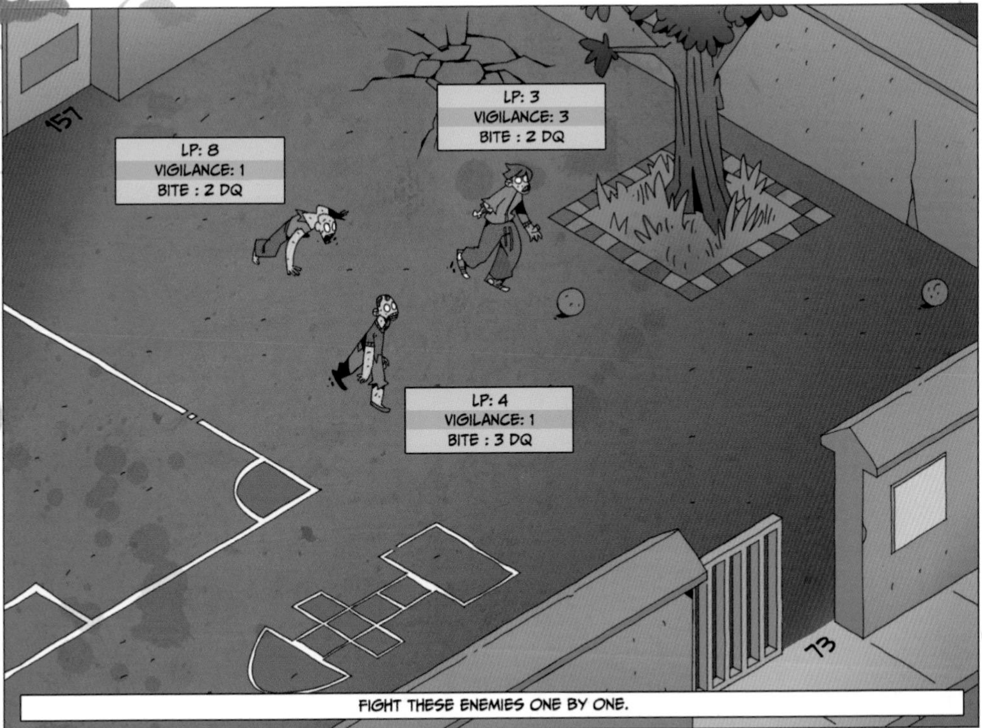

FIGHT THESE ENEMIES ONE BY ONE.

63

383
119

64

248
202

65

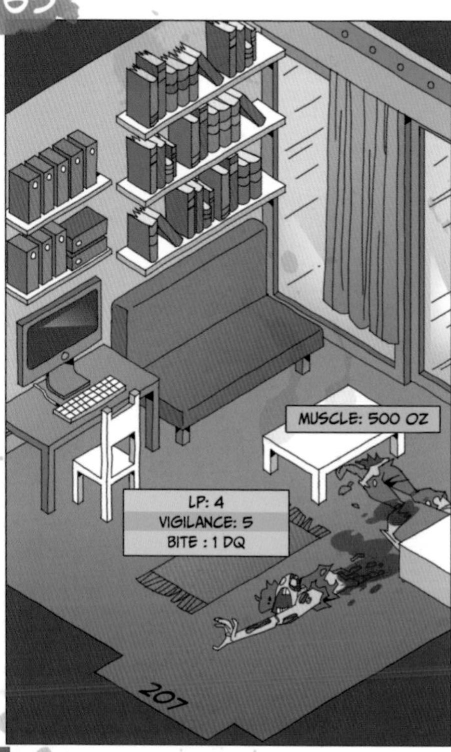
MUSCLE: 500 OZ
LP: 4
VIGILANCE: 5
BITE : 1 DQ
207

66

IT WILL COST YOU 3 LP TO CHASE THESE TWO COLLEAGUES. OR YOU CAN GO BACK TO 153.

67

3
245

68

THANKS FOR THE HELP! BYE!
YOU WON'T BE ABLE TO GET AWAY FROM THIS BUNCH OF ZOMBIES... YOU'RE DEAD.

69

73
LP: 10
VIGILANCE: 7
WEAPON : UMBRELLA (3 DQ, 2 IP)
HEART: 100 OZ
BRAIN: 200 OZ
MUSCLE: 100 OZ
314

70

234

71

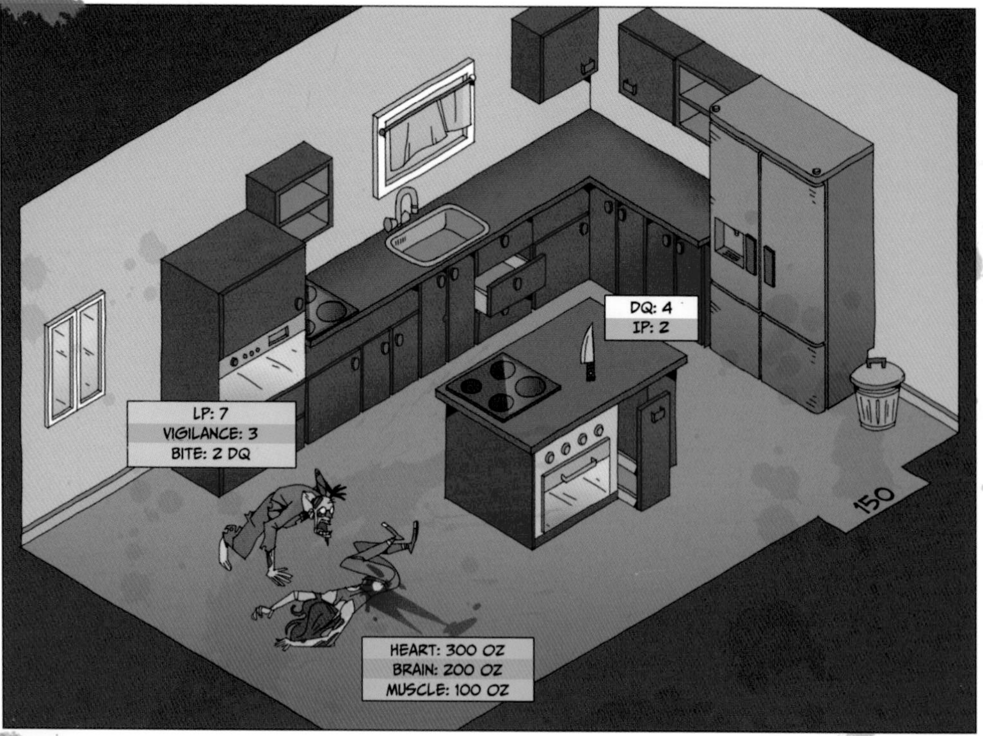

DQ: 4
IP: 2

LP: 7
VIGILANCE: 3
BITE: 2 DQ

150

HEART: 300 OZ
BRAIN: 200 OZ
MUSCLE: 100 OZ

72

246

LP: 7
VIGILANCE: 7
WEAPON: GRILLING FORK (2 DQ, 2 IP)
HEART: 100 OZ
BRAIN: 200 OZ
MUSCLE: 400 OZ

151

73

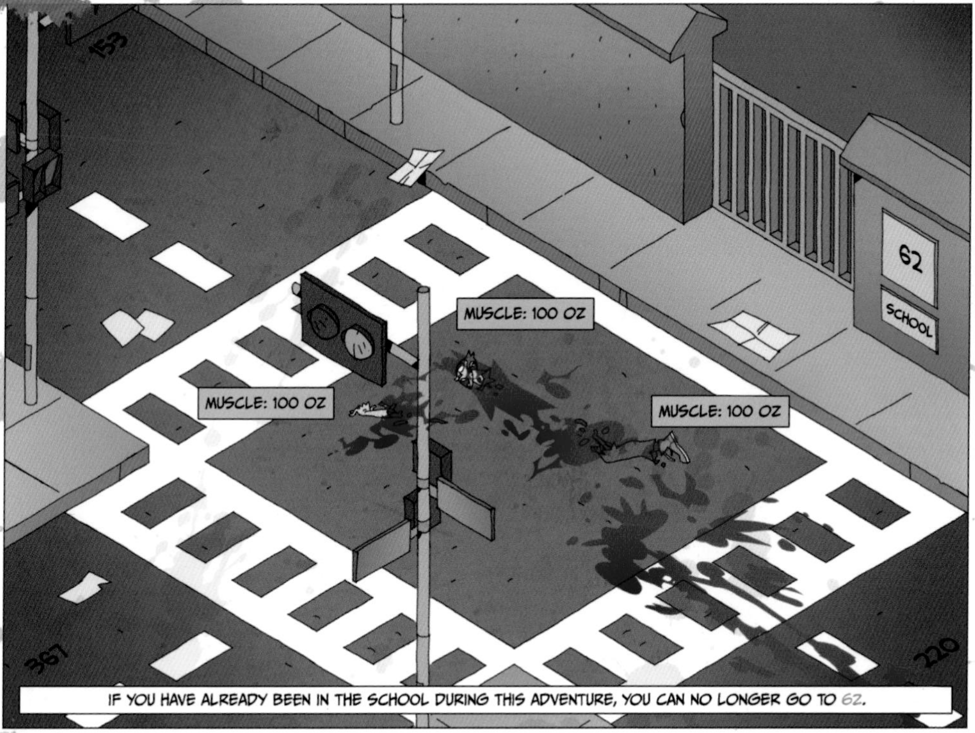

153

62

SCHOOL

MUSCLE: 100 OZ

MUSCLE: 100 OZ

MUSCLE: 100 OZ

367

220

IF YOU HAVE ALREADY BEEN IN THE SCHOOL DURING THIS ADVENTURE, YOU CAN NO LONGER GO TO 62.

74

183

199

263

204

75

160

194

232

76

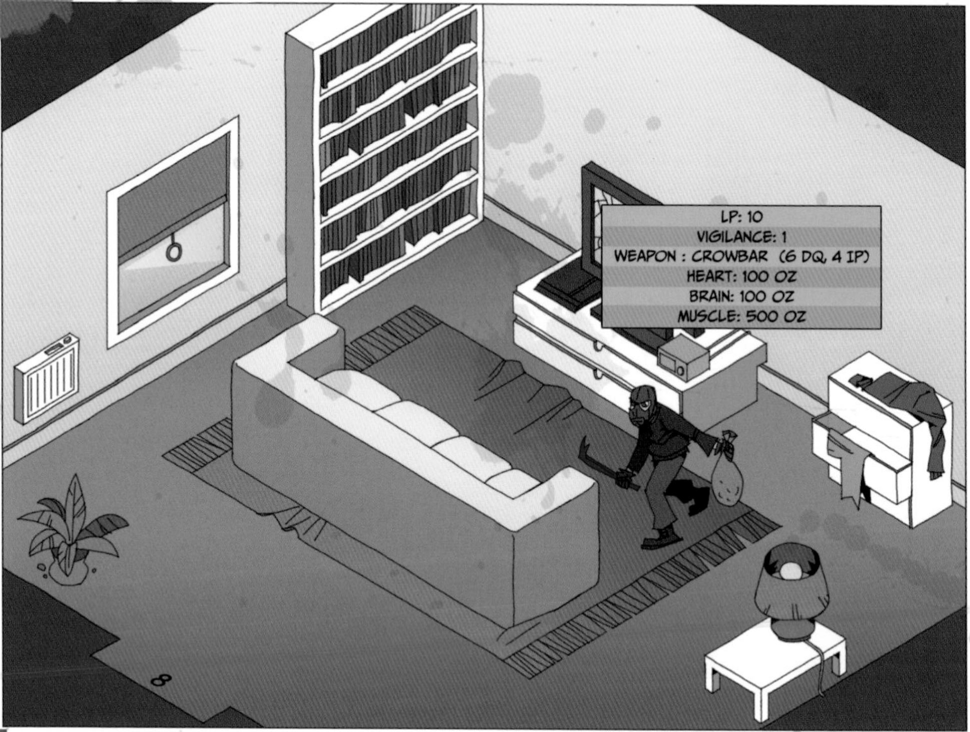

8

77

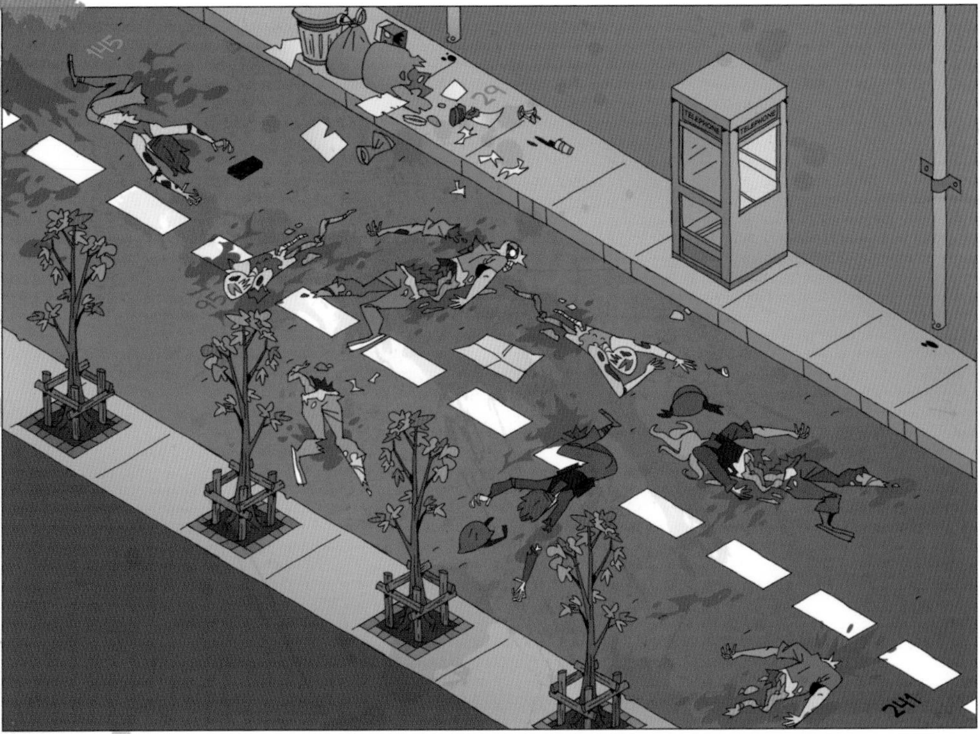

145
29
TELEPHONE
TELEPHONE
95
241

78

291
152
217

79

205

DEMOCRACY
=
ANARCHY

251

195

80

286

350

81

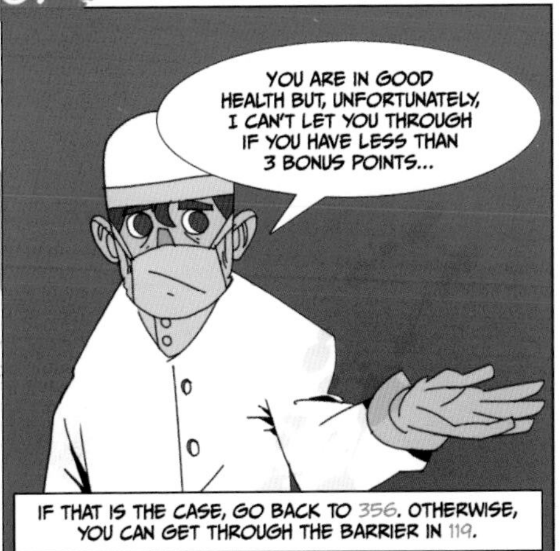

I82

83

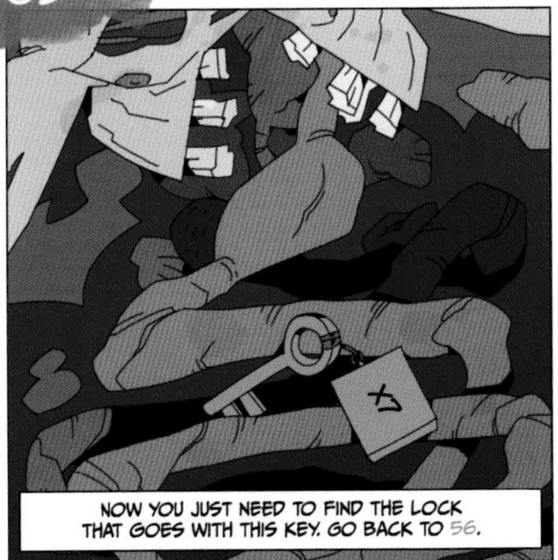

84

C/Q/Z85

X86

87

RATS! THIS FALL MAKES YOU LOSE 10 LP.
GO TO 41 IF YOU ARE STILL ALIVE...

88

315
249

89

LP: 12
VIGILANCE: 7
BITE: 3 DQ
VICTORY-> 109

90

X4X
110

91

229
155
DQ: 3
IP: 2
303

92

310
166
284

93

210
344

94

20
HEART: 200 OZ
BRAIN: 100 OZ
MUSCLE: 50 OZ
360

95

96

K/X97

98

99

100

101

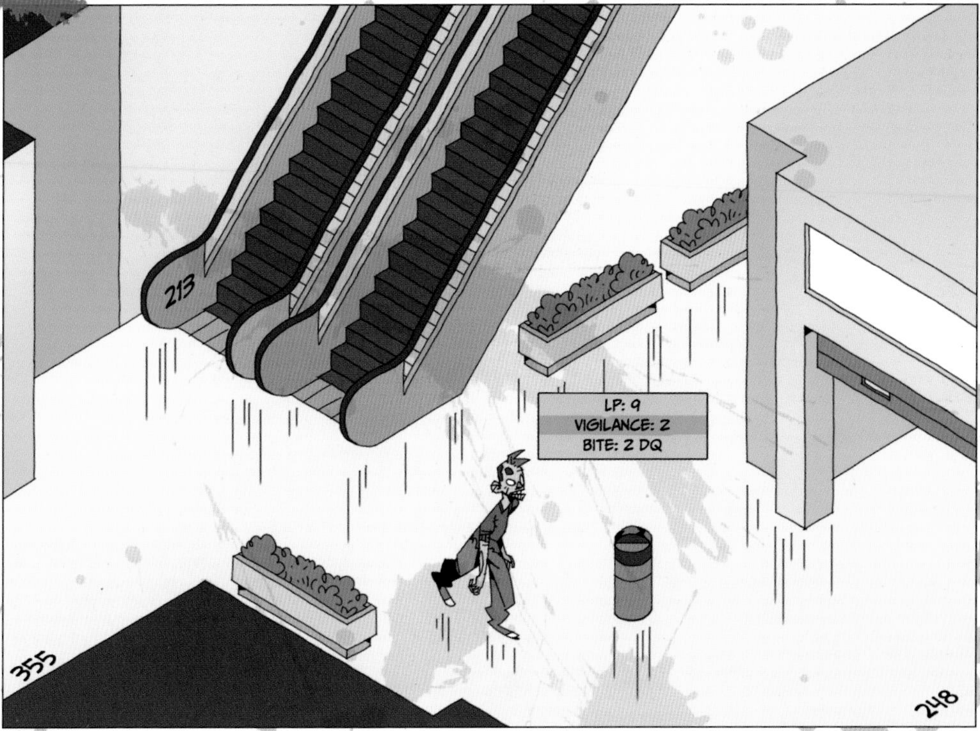

213

LP: 9
VIGILANCE: 2
BITE: 2 DQ

355

248

102

37

314

103

THESE KIDS ARE TOO TERRORIZED FOR YOU TO TAKE THEM WITH YOU. YOU HAVE TO LEAVE THEM HERE... YOU LOSE 1 BONUS POINT FOR HAVING KILLED THEIR FATHER... THESE KIDS ARE TOO TERRORIZED TO DEFEND THEMSELVES. BON APPETITE!

HEART: 1 LB
BRAIN: 1 LB
MUSCLE: 1 LB

GO BACK TO 54.

104

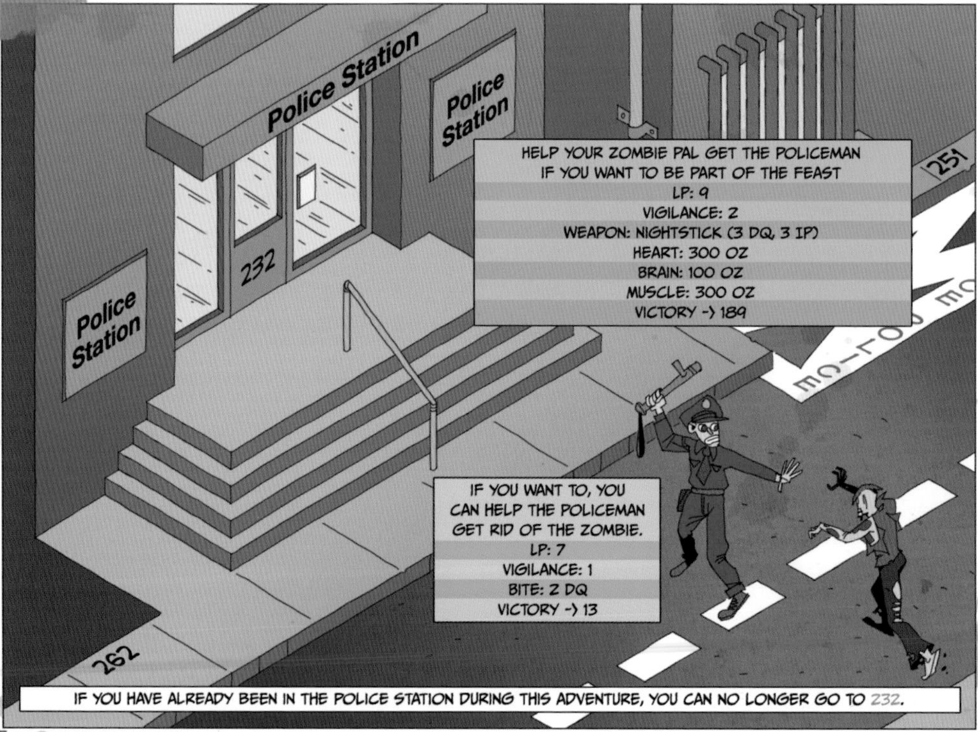

Police Station
Police Station
Police Station
232
262
251

HELP YOUR ZOMBIE PAL GET THE POLICEMAN IF YOU WANT TO BE PART OF THE FEAST

LP: 9
VIGILANCE: 2
WEAPON: NIGHTSTICK (3 DQ, 3 IP)
HEART: 300 OZ
BRAIN: 100 OZ
MUSCLE: 300 OZ
VICTORY -> 189

IF YOU WANT TO, YOU CAN HELP THE POLICEMAN GET RID OF THE ZOMBIE.

LP: 7
VIGILANCE: 1
BITE: 2 DQ
VICTORY -> 13

IF YOU HAVE ALREADY BEEN IN THE POLICE STATION DURING THIS ADVENTURE, YOU CAN NO LONGER GO TO 232.

RAAH
SLPR
SLARCH

SCRUNCH

?!

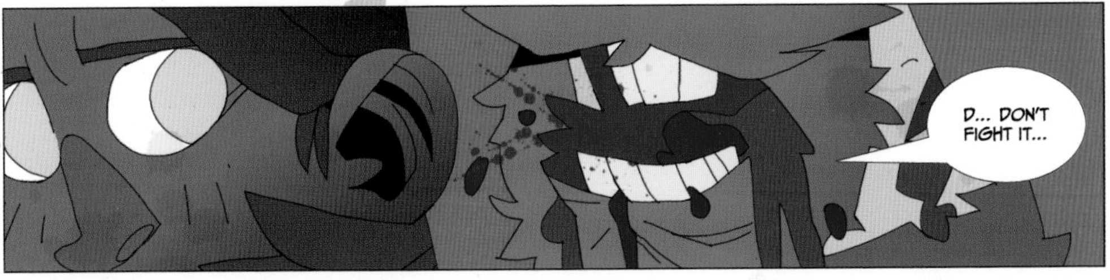
D... DON'T FIGHT IT...

...AND R...RUN WHEN I T...TELL YOU TOO...
THE END

106

202

245

96

107

336

207

THERE IS STILL TIME TO GET OUT OF THE BUILDING THROUGH 112.

108

354

332

109

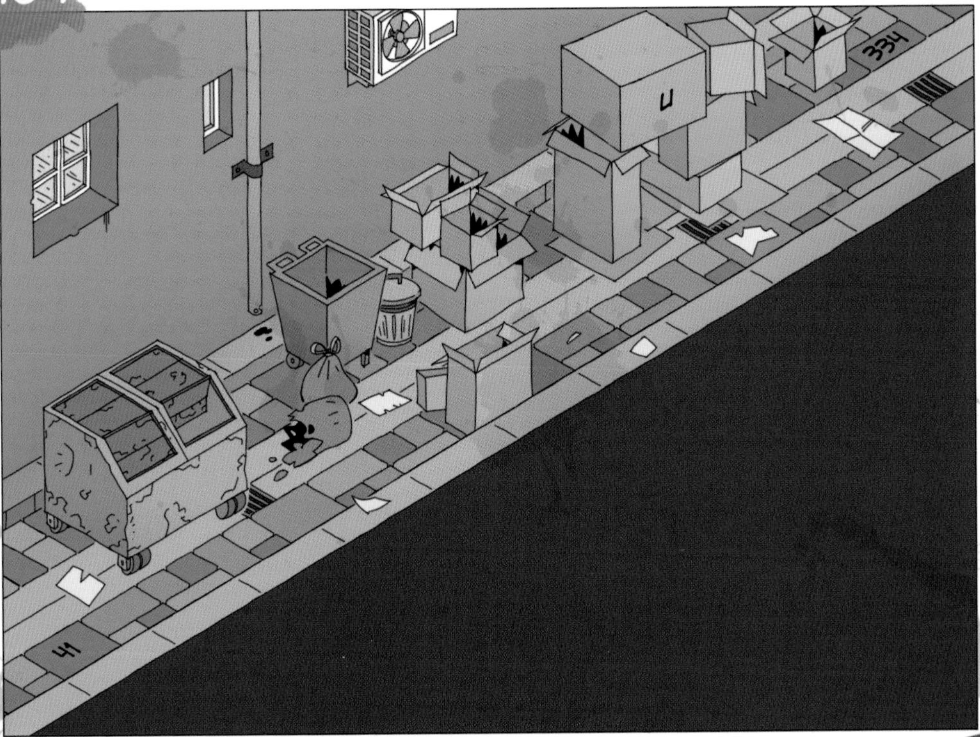

334

41

110

111

112

113

114

THIS ACCIDENT KILLS DENISE AND ONE MORE OF YOUR ALLIES (OR WILL COST YOU 7 LP IF YOU'RE ON YOUR OWN). GET OUT OF THE MINIBUS QUICKLY THROUGH 59 BEFORE THE ZOMBIES FIND YOU!

115

YOU STILL HAVE TIME TO GET AWAY! GO TO 170 IF YOU DON'T FEEL LIKE FIGHTING HIM.

116

117

118

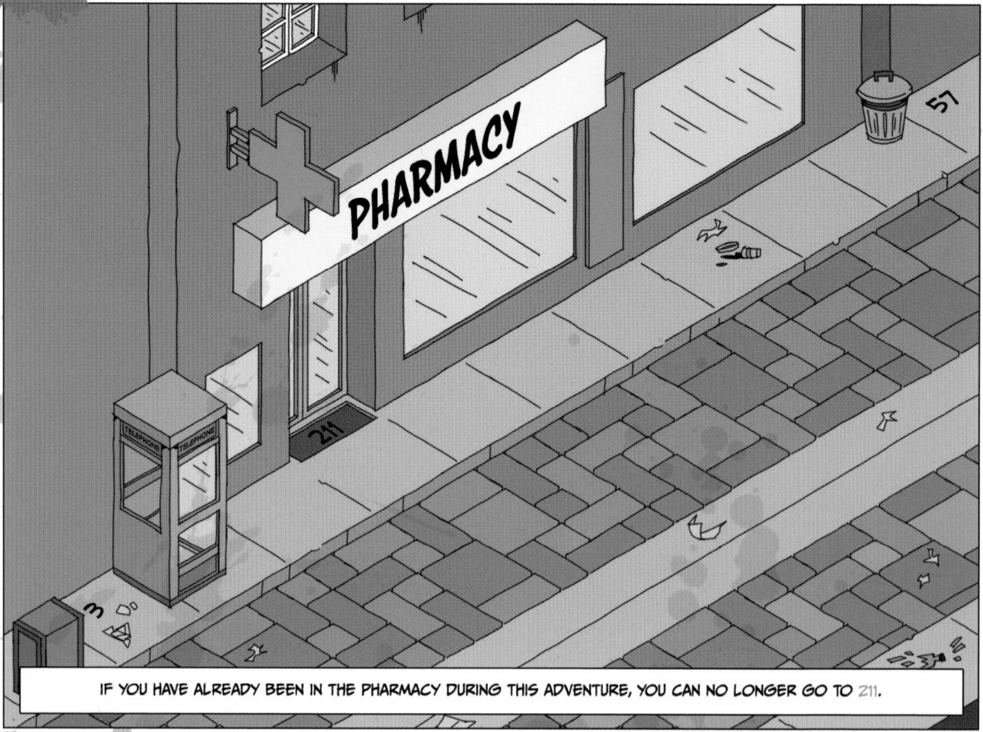

IF YOU HAVE ALREADY BEEN IN THE PHARMACY DURING THIS ADVENTURE, YOU CAN NO LONGER GO TO 211.

119

120

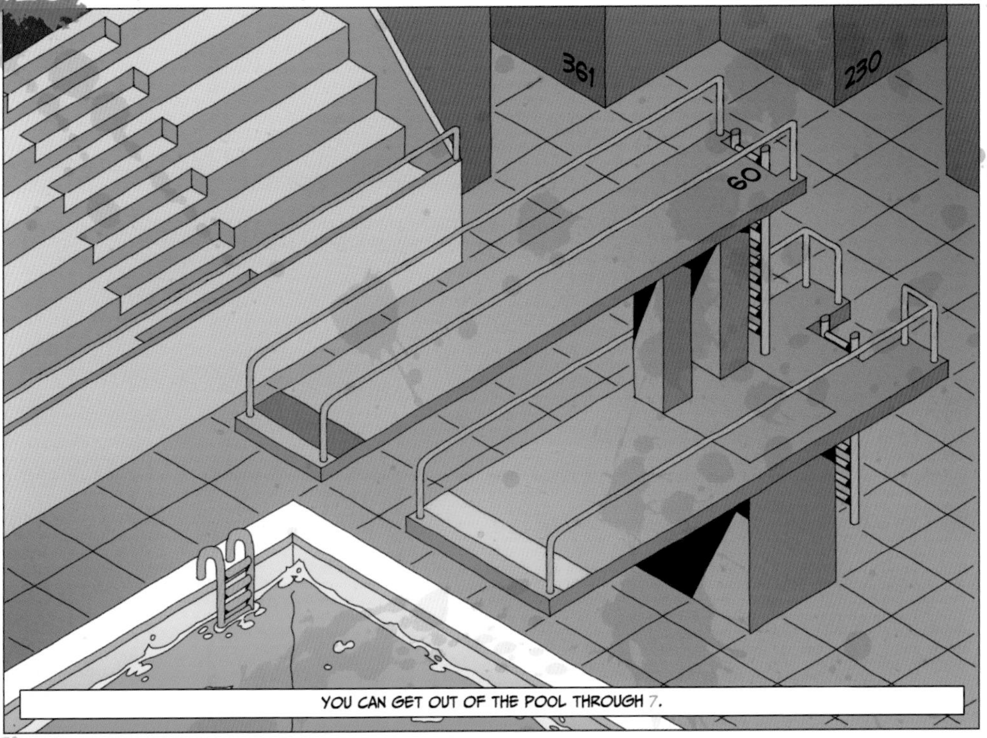

YOU CAN GET OUT OF THE POOL THROUGH 7.

121

YOU CAN ALSO GO BACK TO 170 IF YOU DON'T TRUST THIS GUY.

RAAH RAAAAH

RAAH
RAAAAH

CLAC!

RAAAAH
I'M SORRY...

I MUST SURVIVE..
THE END

123

245

5

124

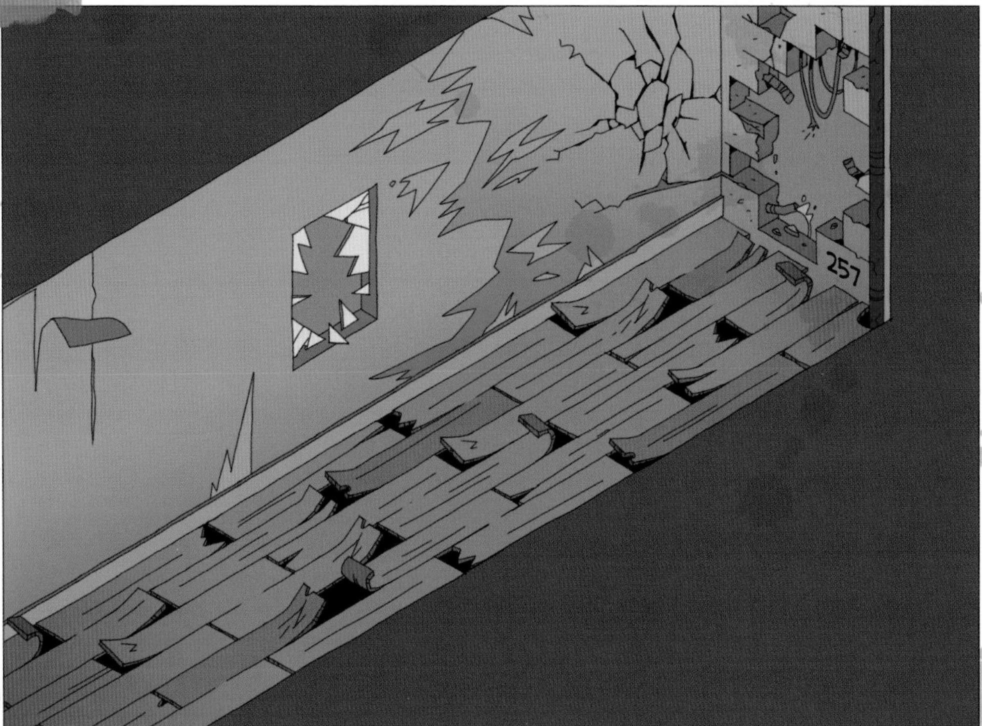

257

LP: 12
VIGILANCE: 8
WEAPON: IRON BAR (5 DQ, 4 IP)
HEART: 200 OZ
BRAIN: 200 OZ
MUSCLE: 300 OZ

378

LP: 30
WEAPON: BEWITCHED DAGGER (10 DQ, 10 IP)
VICTORY -> 173

W127

128

129

A130

131

132

133

134

135

136

137

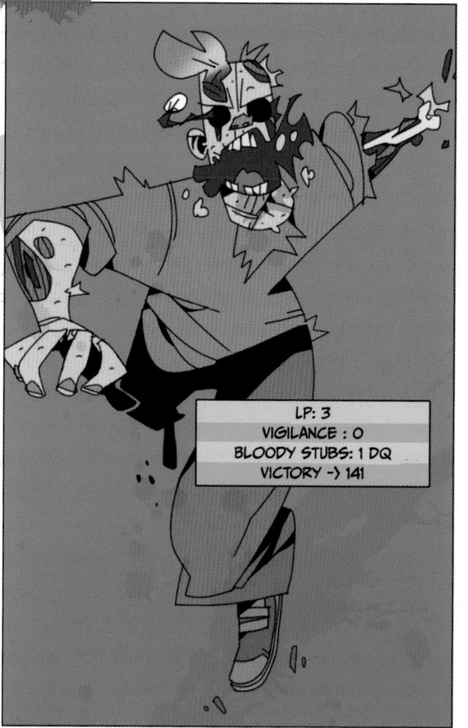

138

139

140

141

THIS FIGHT TAUGHT YOU A BIT MORE ABOUT ZOMBIES, YOU WIN 1 SP. GO BACK TO 3.

142

TAKE ADVANTAGE OF THE DISTRACTION! GO ON TO 80!

143

IF YOU HAVE FEWER THAN 3 IP OR FEWER THAN 3 SP, YOU SLIDE AND FALL TO 117. OTHERWISE GO ON TO 253.

144

IF YOU HAVE AT LEAST 5 OR MORE SP, YOU CAN TRY AND PASS AS ONE OF THEM BY STOMPING AND ROARING. SO GO TO 324. IF NOT, GO TO 275.

145

THIS SURPRISE ATTACK COST YOU THE LIFE OF AN ALLY (OF YOUR CHOICE) OR 7 LP IF YOU'RE ON YOUR OWN. RUN TO 29.

A146

GO TO 113.

147

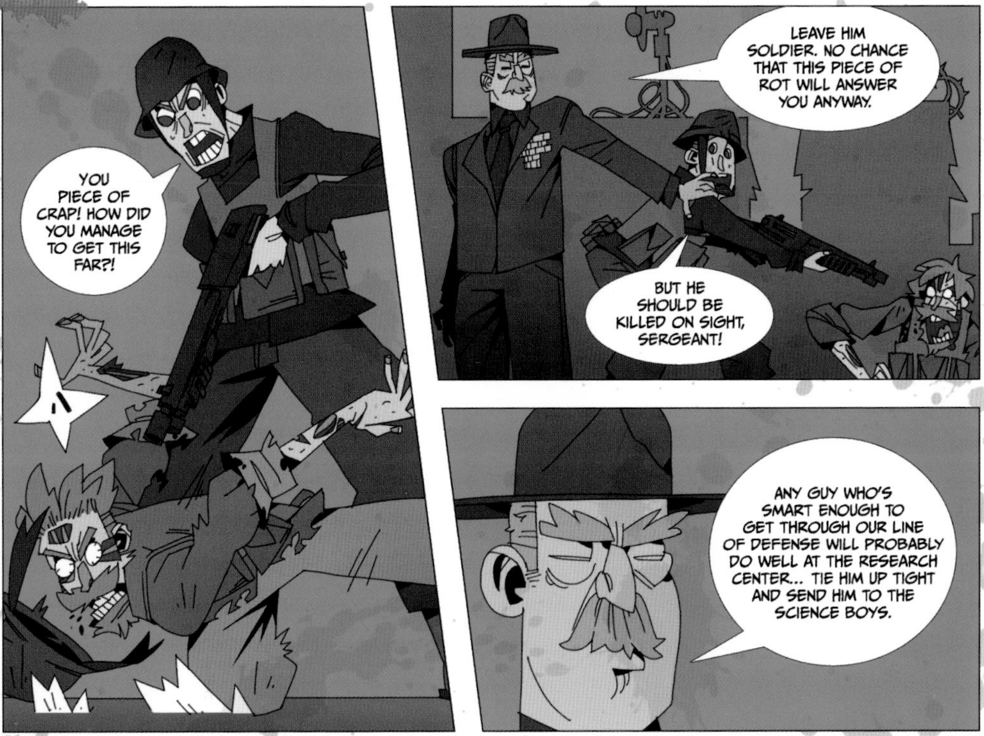

YOU PIECE OF CRAP! HOW DID YOU MANAGE TO GET THIS FAR?!

LEAVE HIM SOLDIER. NO CHANCE THAT THIS PIECE OF ROT WILL ANSWER YOU ANYWAY.

BUT HE SHOULD BE KILLED ON SIGHT, SERGEANT!

ANY GUY WHO'S SMART ENOUGH TO GET THROUGH OUR LINE OF DEFENSE WILL PROBABLY DO WELL AT THE RESEARCH CENTER... TIE HIM UP TIGHT AND SEND HIM TO THE SCIENCE BOYS.

247

323

LP: 3
VIGILANCE: 4
BITES: 2 DQ

LP: 4
VIGILANCE: 3
STUBS: 1 DQ

LP: 2
VIGILANCE: 3
BITES: 3 DQ

LP: 5
VIGILANCE: 5
STUBS: 2 DQ

FIGHT THESE ENEMIES ONE AT A TIME.

149

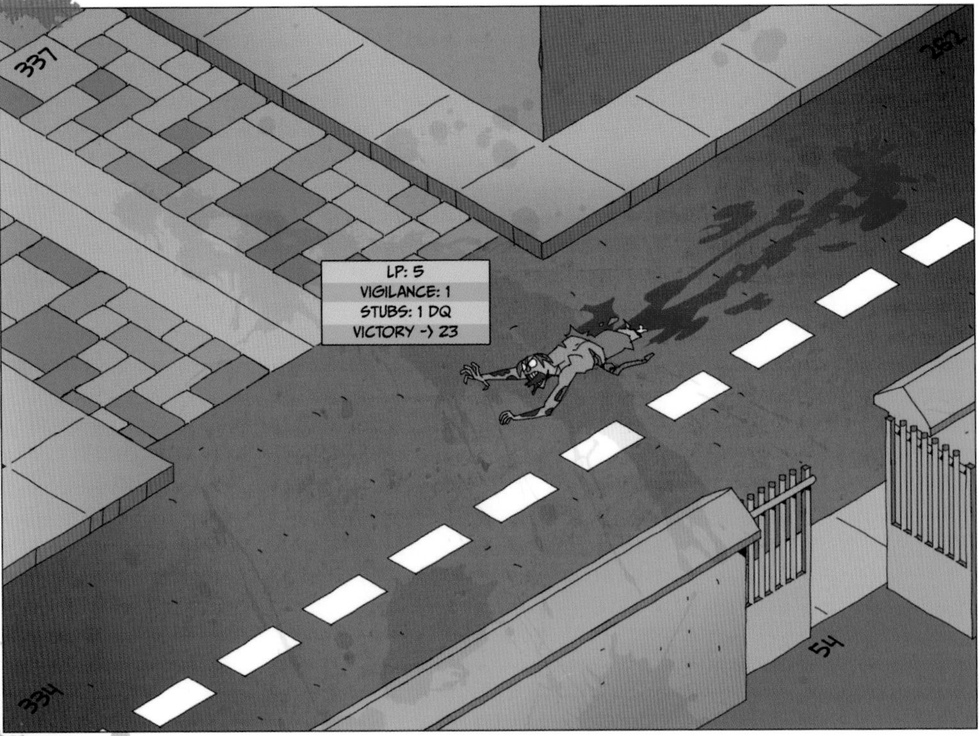

337

282

LP: 5
VIGILANCE: 1
STUBS: 1 DQ
VICTORY -> 23

54

334

150

71

328

376

151

LP: 4
VIGILANCE: 3
STUBS: 1 DQ

22
212
72

152

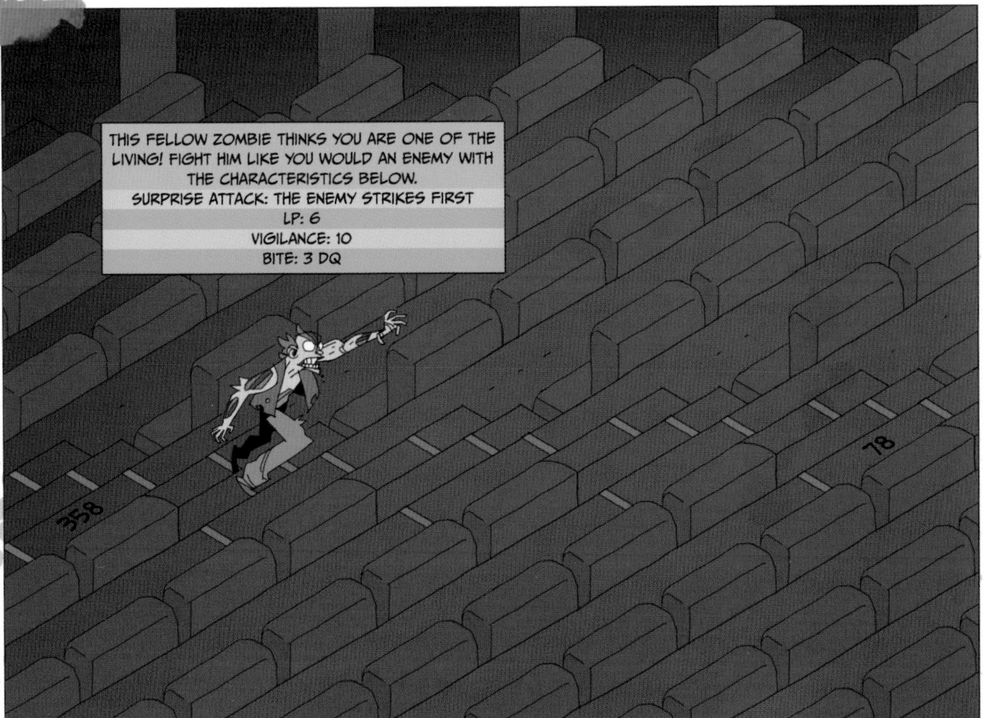

THIS FELLOW ZOMBIE THINKS YOU ARE ONE OF THE LIVING! FIGHT HIM LIKE YOU WOULD AN ENEMY WITH THE CHARACTERISTICS BELOW.
SURPRISE ATTACK: THE ENEMY STRIKES FIRST
LP: 6
VIGILANCE: 10
BITE: 3 DQ

358
78

153

371

73

154

RUN...
RUN!

258

280

367

155

318

91

226

368

229

156

299

369

HEART: 300 OZ
BRAIN: 200 OZ
MUSCLE: 100 OZ

20

157

158

159

160

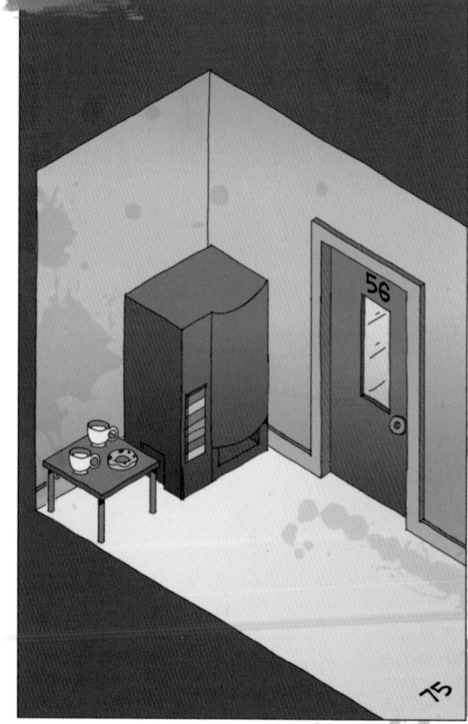

161

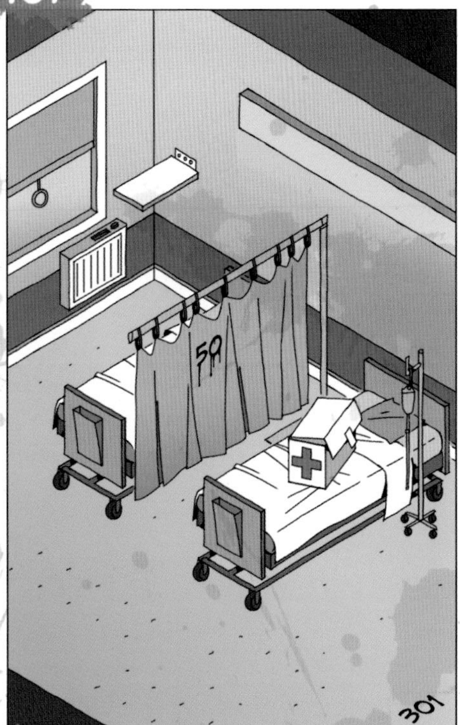

162

163

164

165

272

292

343

379

166

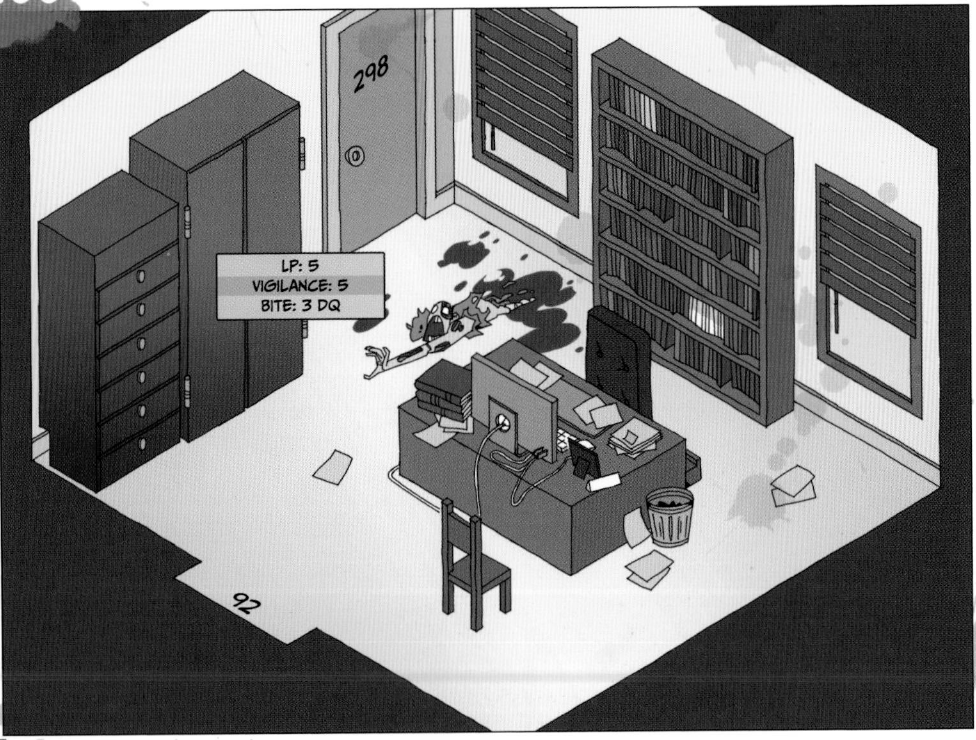

298

LP: 5
VIGILANCE: 5
BITE: 3 DQ

92

167

GO AHEAD, HELP YOURSELF!

ONCE YOU HAVE FILLED YOUR BAG, GO BACK TO 170.

168

ZI END

EVEN THOUGH THE FILM WAS TERRIBLE, YOU LEARNED A LOT ABOUT WHAT TO DO IN THE EVENT OF AN INVASION. YOU GET 3 SP OR 3 IP AND GO BACK TO 217.

SCRUNCH

BVRRRRRRRRR
SLARCH
SLPR

RRRRRRRRK

FWIIIIIIIIIIII
THE END

170

PET STORE

PET STORE

302

213

6

256

171

THIS IS VERY HELPFUL! YOU GET A PERMANENT 1 DQ. UNFORTUNATELY, THERE'S NOT ENOUGH TIME DO TO MORE RESEARCH. GET OUT THROUGH 18.

172

249

303

173

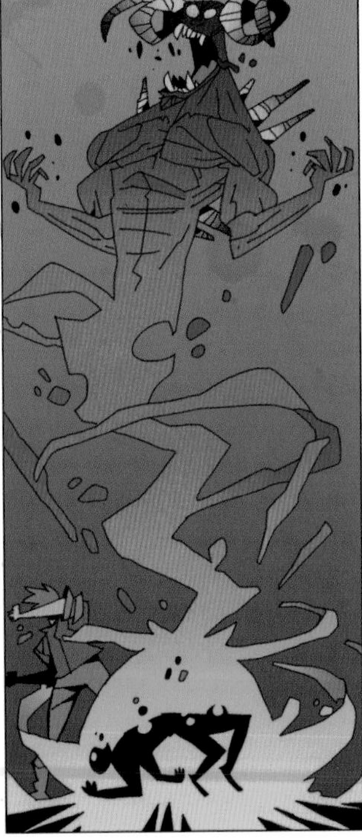

174

175

THIS FIGHT AGAINST A LIVING BEING TOUGHENED YOU UP. YOU GET 2 SP. GO TO 133.

K176

Z177

178

179

180

181

THEY'VE BLOCKED US. WE HAVE TO TRY AND GET OUT IN 31 BEFORE THEY'VE COMPLETELY SURROUNDED US!

10

182

183

184

185

186

187

188

NOW YOU JUST NEED TO FIND THE LOCK THAT GOES WITH THIS KEY. BY THE WAY, YOU CAN ONLY USE IT IF YOU HAVE 5 IP AT THE TIME (TAKE NOTE OF THIS).
GO BACK TO 172.

189

NOW YOU JUST NEED TO FIND THE LOCK THAT GOES WITH THIS KEY. BY THE WAY, YOU CAN ONLY USE IT IF YOU HAVE 5 IP AT THE TIME (TAKE NOTE OF THIS).
GO BACK TO 104.

190

GUN: 7 DQ
AM: 3

TO SHOOT, GO TO 322.
IF YOU DON'T HAVE THE COURAGE, GO TO 113.

Q191

THE KID'S BEEN CAUGHT!
TO HELP HIM WILL ONLY CONDEMN YOU...
MOVE ON WITHOUT HIM TO 38.

192

HEART: 300 OZ
BRAIN: 300 OZ
MUSCLES: 300 OZ

YOU CAN CHASE OFF THIS ZOMBIE IN ORDER TO TAKE ADVANTAGE OF YOUR KILL, BUT YOU LEAVE 2 LP BEHIND.
ONCE YOU'VE HAD ENOUGH GO TO 241.

193

MAKE NOTE OF IT AND GO TO 264.

194

I... I DON'T KNOW WHAT TO DO! THIS GUY DOESN'T LOOK AGGRESSIVE, BUT NO ONE CAN SURVIVE THAT KIND OF WOUND... SHOULD I SHOOT HIM OR NOT?

YOU DON'T KNOW EITHER. GO BACK TO 75.

195

315

LP: 8
VIGILANCE: 2
WEAPON: PEN (2 DQ, 1 IP)
HEART: 300 OZ
BRAIN: 200 OZ
MUSCLES: 100 OZ

353

IF YOU HAVE ALREADY BEEN IN THE TOWN HALL ON THIS ADVENTURE, YOU CAN NO LONGER GO TO 353.

196

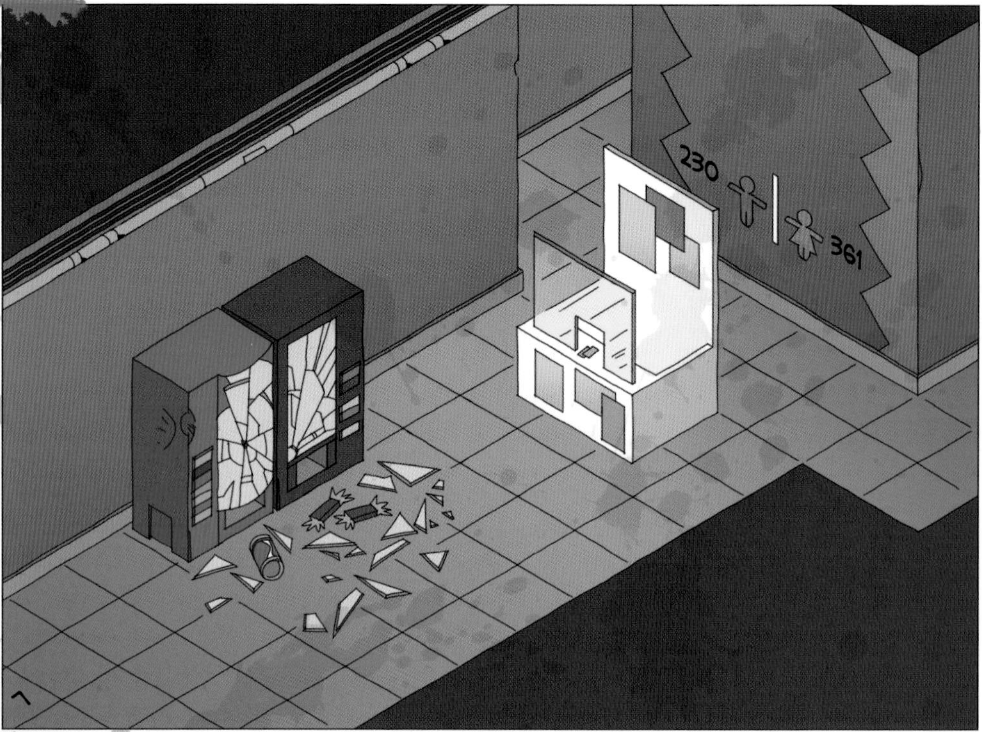

197

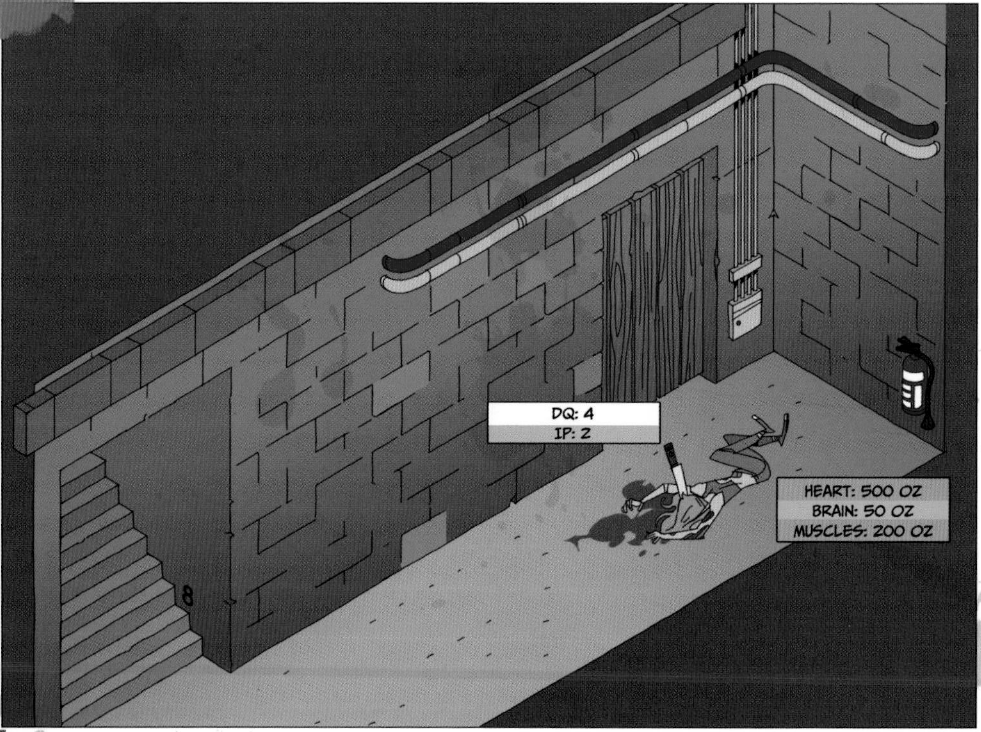

198

285

213

199

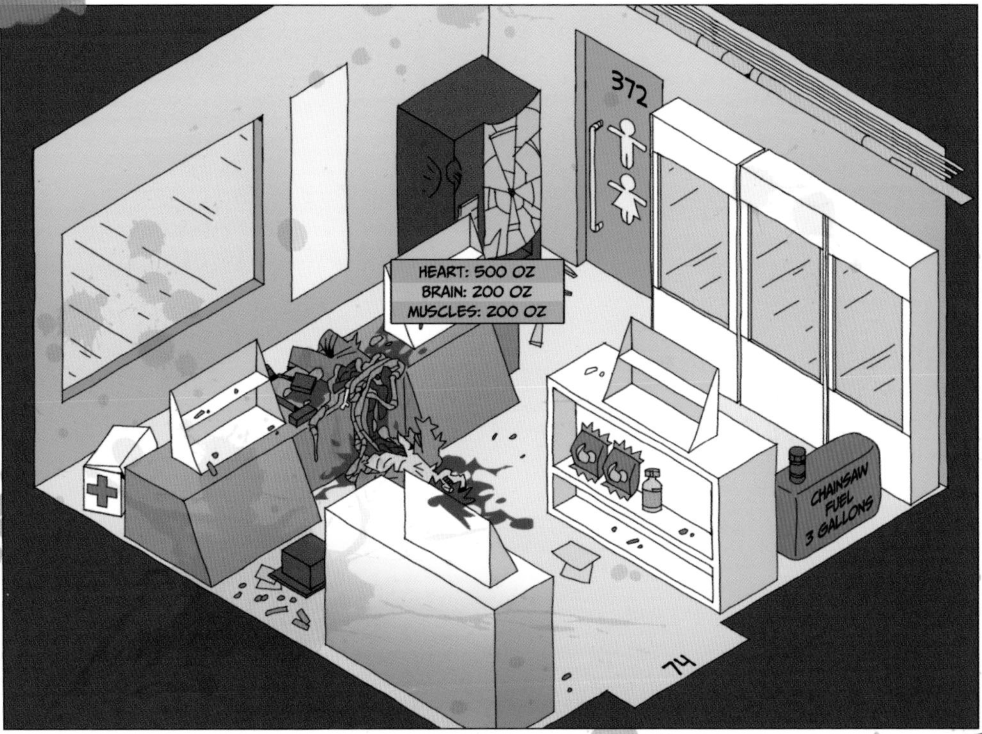

372

HEART: 500 OZ
BRAIN: 200 OZ
MUSCLES: 200 OZ

CHAINSAW FUEL 3 GALLONS

74

HOSPITAL

PUBLIC POOL

MULTIPLEX CINEMA

POLICE STATION

TOWN HALL

SHOPPING CENTER

YOU ARE HERE!

PUBLIC SCHOOL

PUBLIC GARDEN

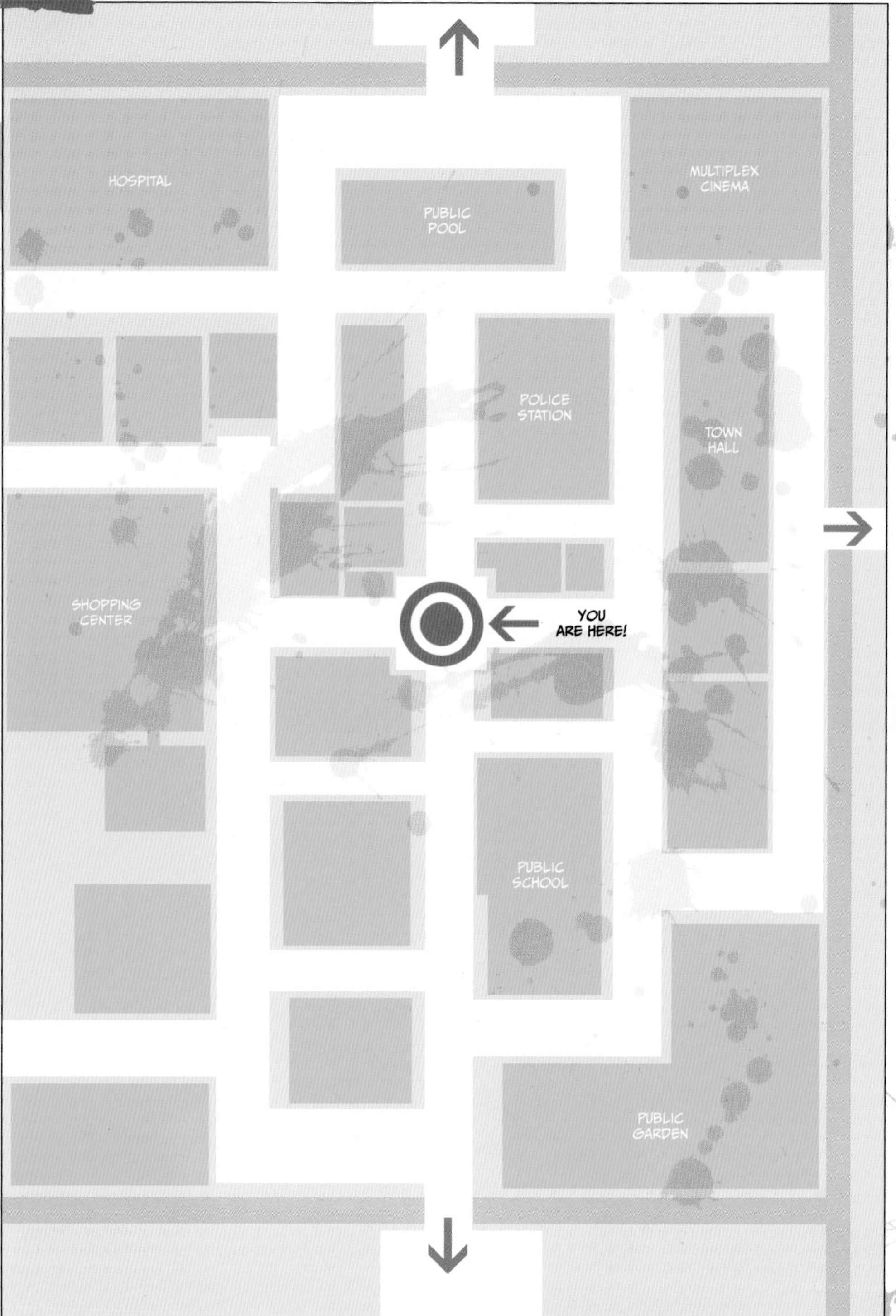

TO GET OUT OF TOWN YOU NEED TO GET TO ONE OF THE EXITS MARKED WITH AN ARROW ON THE MAP. SO THAT YOU CAN REFER BACK TO IT FROM TIME TO TIME, NOTE THE NUMBER IN YOUR JOURNAL (WHICH YOU CAN ALSO DOWNLOAD FROM *IDWPUBLISHING.COM/ZOMBIE-THE-ADVENTURE-IS-YOURS/*). NOW, GO BACK TO 3.

201

354
108

202

106
64

LP: 6
VIGILANCE: 2
UMBRELLA: 3 DQ

LP: 12
VIGILANCE:
WEAPON: KNIFE (4 DQ, 2 IP)
HEART: 100 OZ
BRAIN: 200 OZ
MUSCLES: 100 OZ

183

203

204

205

206

207

208

209

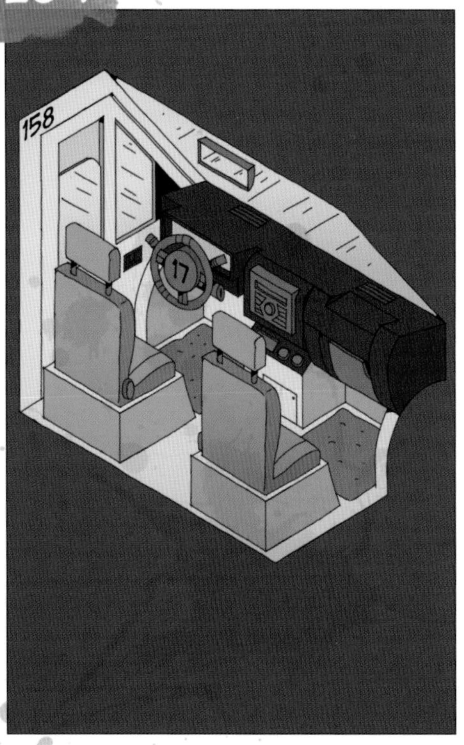

210

211

118

212

HEY! YOU THERE! HELP ME PLEASE (1221)!

151

135

213

BAKERY

140

26

101

170

198

357

215

307

40

216

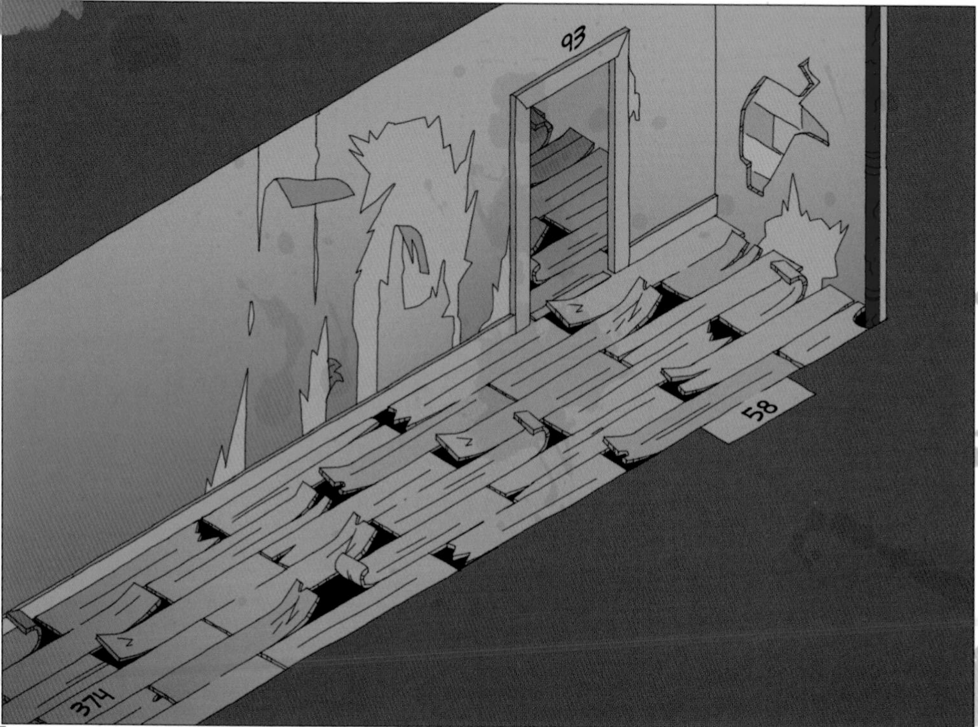

93

58

374

217

78

255

315

218

219

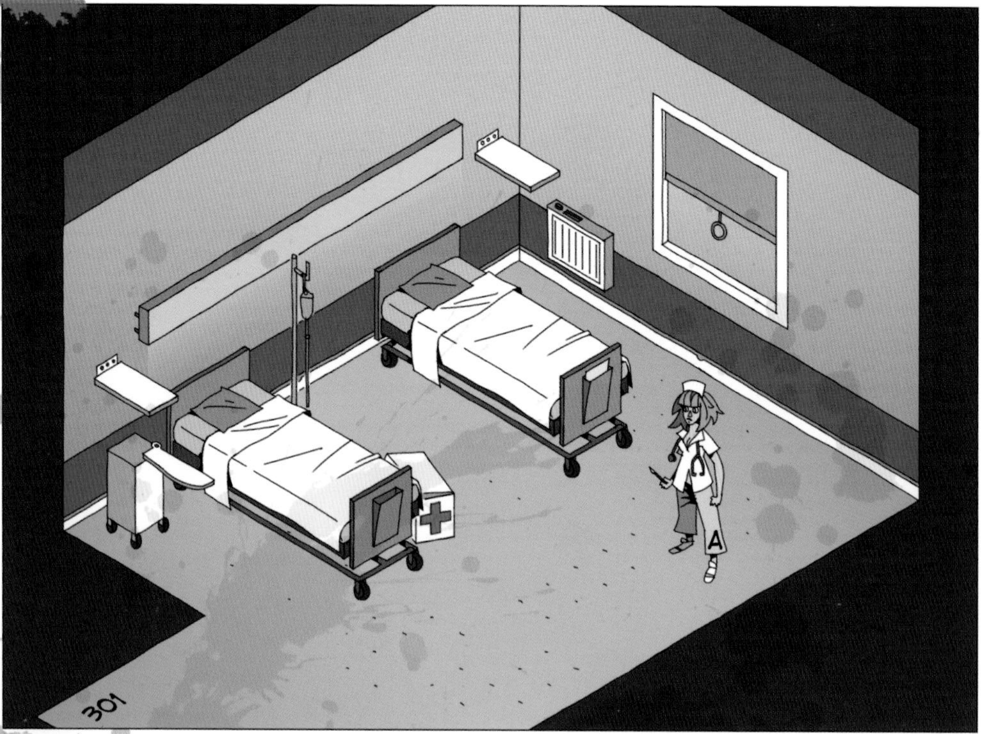

A

301

220

73

135

356

IF YOU HAVE LESS THAN 3 IP GO TO 45.
OTHERWISE, TAKE ANYONE ALIVE AND GO WHEREVER YOU WANT!

221

222

223

224

225

226

227

228

229

230

231

232

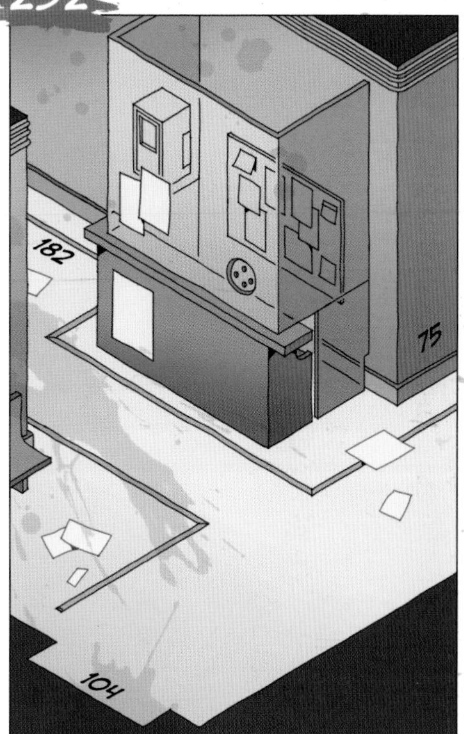

233

234

235

YOUR FELLOW ZOMBIE'S FLESH GETS TO YOUR GUTS... YOU LOSE 3 BONUS POINTS! GO BACK TO 109.

236

YOU HAVE TO FORCE YOUR WAY THROUGH THE CROWD. YOU LOSE 3 LP IN THE EFFORT. CONTINUE ON TO 222.

A237

YOU HAVE NO CHOICE, YOU HAVE TO TAKE THIS PERSON WITH YOU IN YOUR GROUP OR LEAVE ANDREA BEHIND AS WELL! ***NEED TO KNOW:*** SHE CAN ONLY TAKE CARE OF ONE ALLY AT A TIME, IF OTHERS NEED HER HELP YOU ARE GOING TO HAVE TO CHOOSE WHICH ONES GET LEFT BEHIND. GO BACK TO 333.

Z/Q238

YOU CAN'T TAKE TWO KIDS WITH YOU IN YOUR GROUP. ONCE YOU HAVE CHOSEN ONE, GO BACK TO WHERE YOU CAME FROM (Q OR Z).

239

LP: 9
VIGILANCE: 7
BITE: 2 DQ
VICTORY -) 80

240

YOU CAN TRUST ONE OF YOUR ALLIES TO THIS BIKER. YOU WILL NO LONGER HAVE THE SKILLS, BUT YOU CAN KEEP THE BONUS POINTS AND THE WEAPON. MAKE YOUR CHOICE AND GO TO 74.

241

116

77

HELP YOUR ZOMBIE PAL IN HIS FIGHT
LP: 12
VIGILANCE: 1
WEAPON: GUN (7 DQ, 3 AM, 5 IP)
VICTORY -> 192

TO HELP THE SOLDIER YOU NEED TO BEAT THE ZOMBIE
LP:15
VIGILANCE: 1
BITE: 3 DQ
VICTORY -> 224

309

162

242

22

164

HEART: 200 OZ
BRAIN: 400 OZ
MUSCLE: 50 OZ

314

243

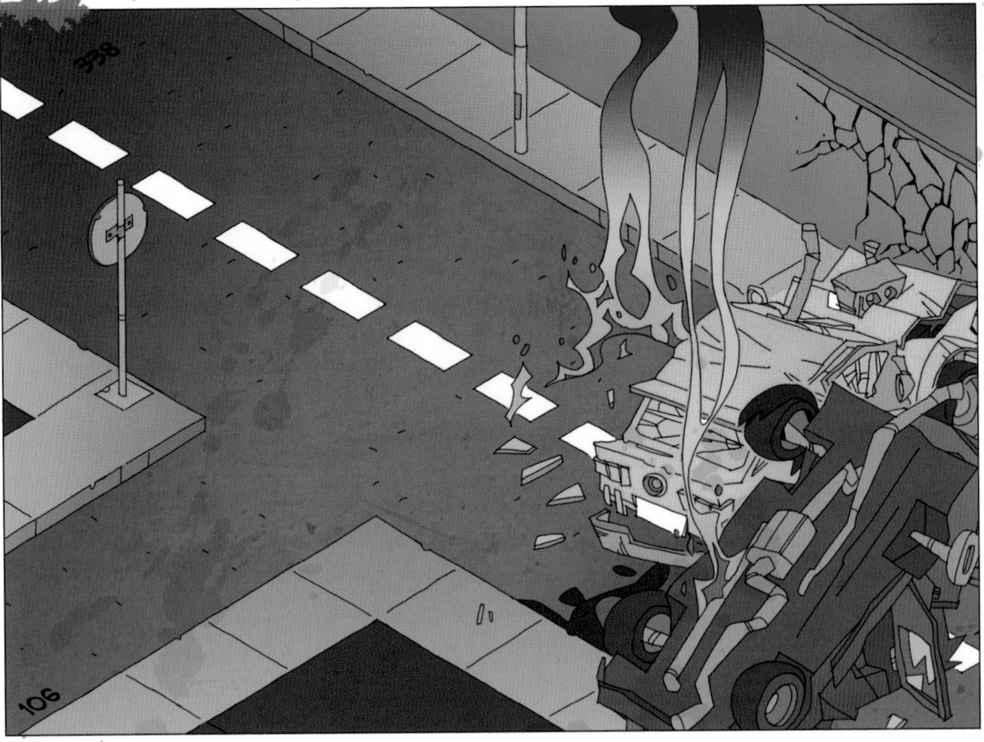

338

106

244

HEART: 1 LB
BRAIN: 1 LB
MUSCLE: 1 LB

THE FEEDING FRENZY AFTER DISCOVERING THE CADAVERS GOT YOU OVER
1 LB OF FLESH (BUT ONLY FOR THIS PANEL). ENJOY! THEN LEAVE THE HOSPITAL IN 180.

245

LP: 4
VIGILANCE: 0
HAMMER: 3 DQ

67

123

337

IF YOU HAVE ALREADY BEEN IN THE CLOTHING STORE DURING YOUR ADVENTURE, YOU CAN NO LONGER GO TO 123.

246

LP: 8
VIGILANCE: 3
KNIFE: 4 DQ

303

72

159

247

159

30

148

248

101

101

163

LP: 3
VIGILANCE: 1
BROOM HANDLE: 2 DQ

64

20

IF YOU HAVE ALREADY BEEN IN THE SHOPPING CENTER DURING YOUR ADVENTURE, YOU CAN NO LONGER GO TO 101.

249

88

LP: 12
VIGILANCE: 5
WEAPON: GUN
(7 DQ, 3 AM, 5 IP)
HEART: 500 OZ
BRAIN: 200 OZ
MUSCLE: 500 OZ

99

370

172

IF YOU HAVE MORE THAN 2 IP YOU'RE SMART ENOUGH TO TAKE THIS SOLDIER BY SURPRISE AND TO TAKE HALF OF HIS LP WITH YOUR FIRST BLOW.

250

D

187

251

252

253

254

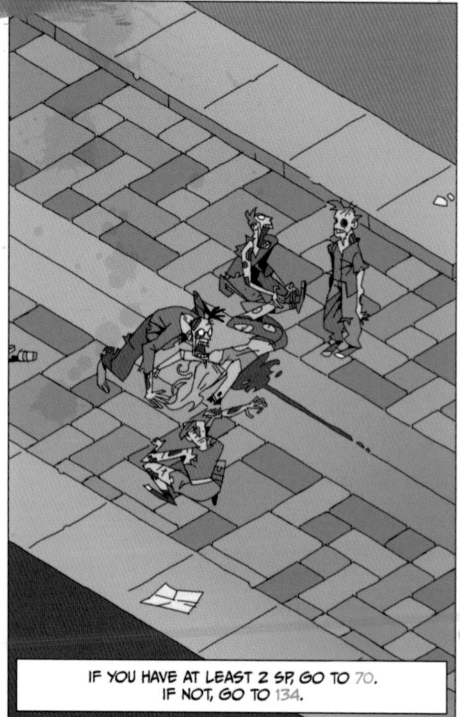

255

GO BACK TO 217.

256

257

258

SPLASH
RATATAK

RATATATATAK
HURRY! YOU STILL HAVE TIME TO JUMP ON!
SPLASH

RATATATAK

STOMP

THE END

260

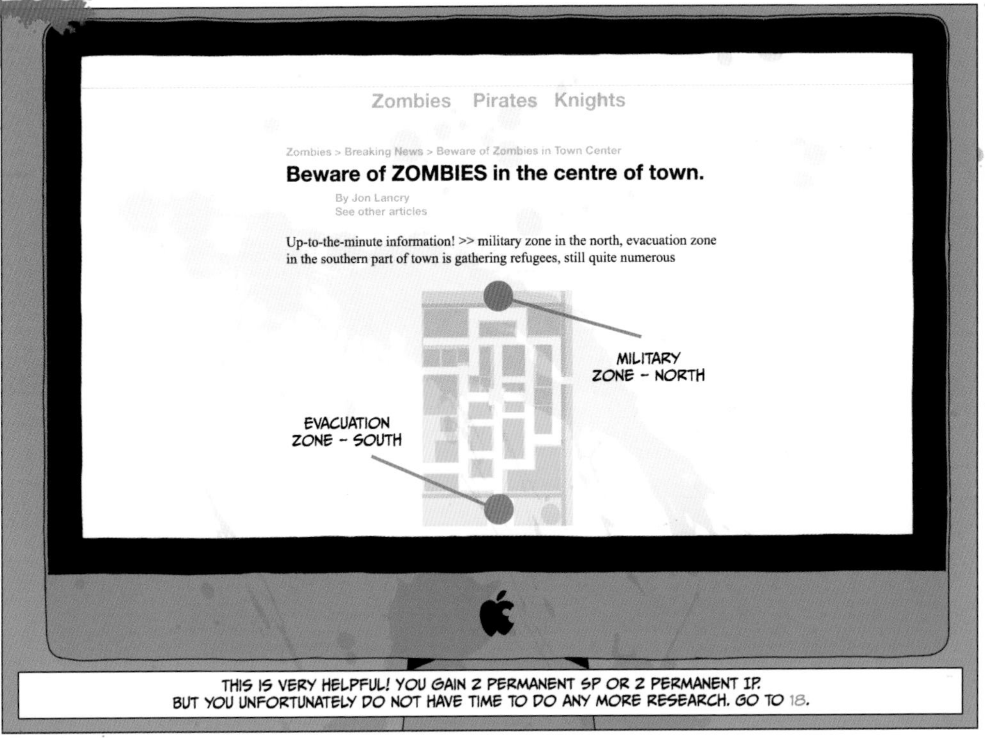

Zombies Pirates Knights

Zombies > Breaking News > Beware of Zombies in Town Center

Beware of ZOMBIES in the centre of town.

By Jon Lancry
See other articles

Up-to-the-minute information! >> military zone in the north, evacuation zone in the southern part of town is gathering refugees, still quite numerous

MILITARY ZONE – NORTH

EVACUATION ZONE – SOUTH

THIS IS VERY HELPFUL! YOU GAIN 2 PERMANENT SP OR 2 PERMANENT IP.
BUT YOU UNFORTUNATELY DO NOT HAVE TIME TO DO ANY MORE RESEARCH. GO TO 18.

261

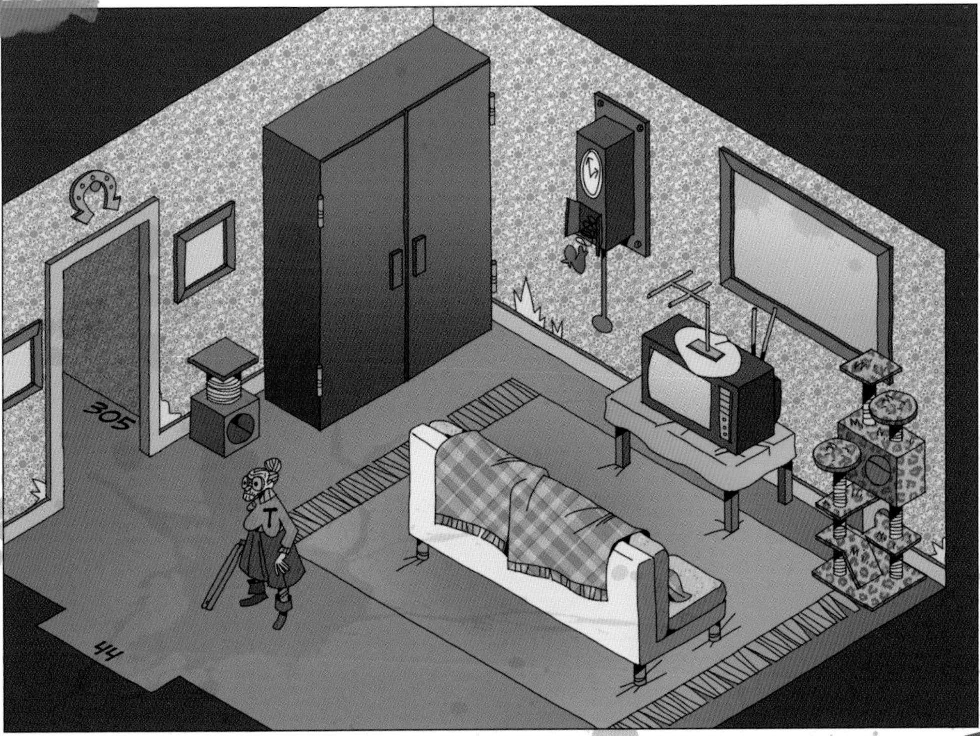

305

44

262

HEART: 300 OZ
BRAIN: 100 OZ
MUSCLE: 50 OZ

104

149

263

YOU HAVE TO PUSH YOUR ZOMBIE COLLEAGUE OUT OF THE WAY FOR TRYING TO EAT THE YUMMY BIKER. THAT WILL COST YOU 5 LP. GO TO PANEL J.

LP: 9
VIGILANCE: 2
BITE: 3 DQ
VICTORY -) J

YOU COULD ALSO GO BACK THROUGH 74.

264

55

265

CATS FOR ALL

CATS FOR ALL

183

378

165

266

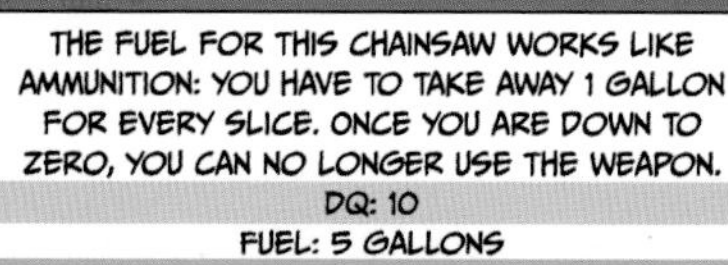

YOU CAN'T TAKE ANYTHING ELSE HERE. GET OUT THROUGH 125. YOU WILL NOT GET ANOTHER CHANCE TO COME BACK TO THE STORE.

267

IF YOU WANT TO KEEP THIS GUY, YOU CAN'T TAKE ANY OTHER MALE CHARACTER... MAKE A NOTE OR MAKE A CHOICE. IF YOU ARE NOT ALONE, THEN GO BACK TO 75.

268

GET OUT OF THE STORE THROUGH 55.

269

WELL, I HATE TO TELL YOU THAT NO ZOMBIE HAS SURVIVED A SHOT TO THE HEAD AT CLOSE RANGE... YOU'RE DEAD.

270

271

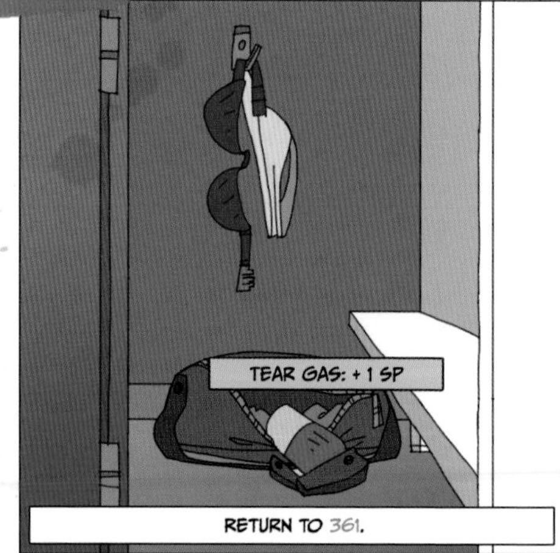

RETURN TO 361.

272

273

C274

275

276

277

278

279

280

281

282

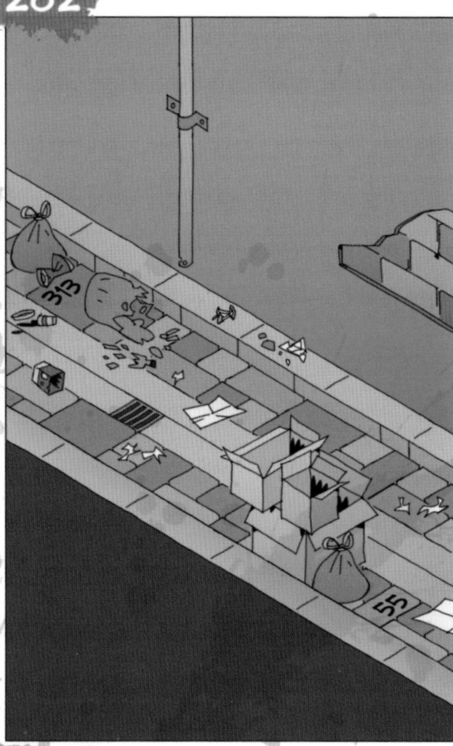

283

284

285

286

287

288

289

290

291

292

X293

294

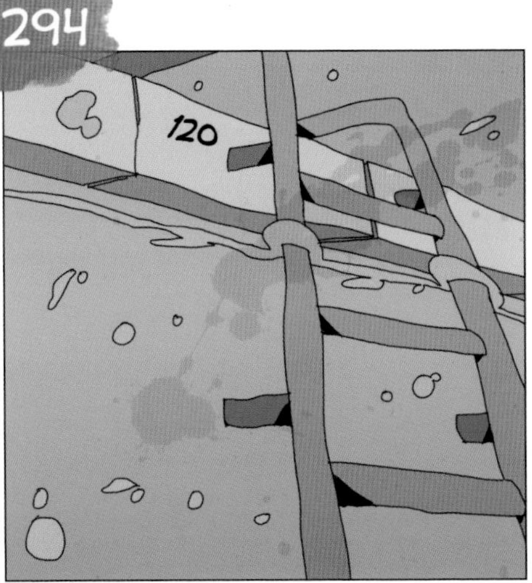

295

296

297

298

YOU STILL HAVE TIME TO GET OUT OF THE BUILDING THROUGH 195.

299

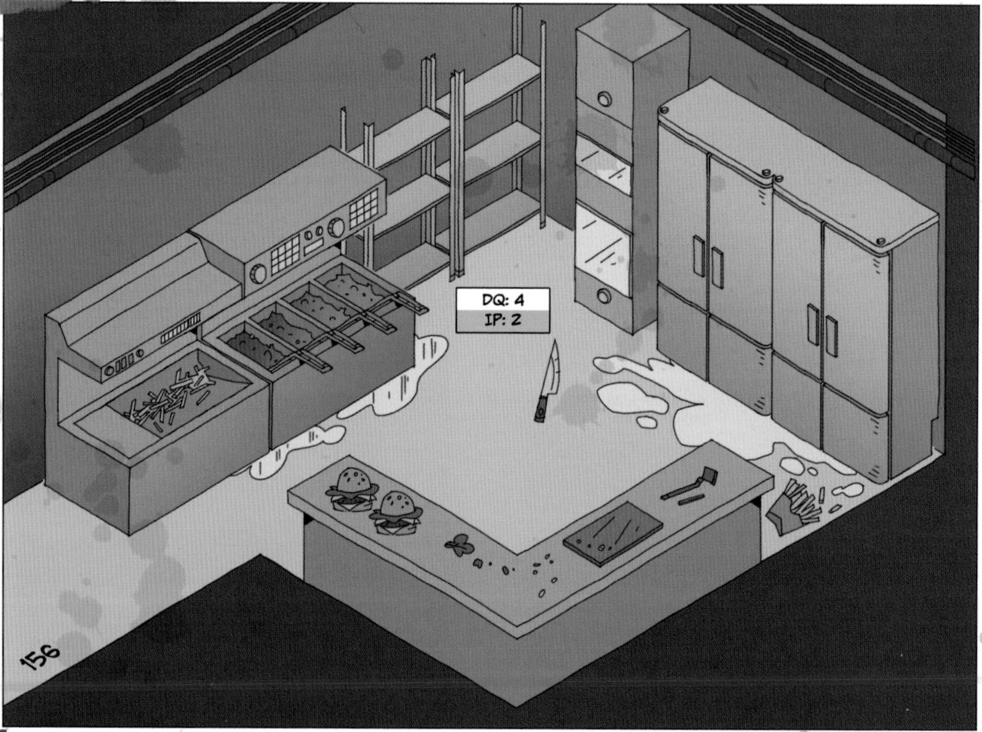

DQ: 4
IP: 2

156

300

ZOMBIES! ON SALE NOW!

185

READING THESE COMICS WILL TEACH YOU MORE ABOUT ZOMBIES.

163

301

161

219

27

302

Y

170

303

172

91

246

SCRUNCH
SLURCH
MÂCH
CROC SLPR
MIOM
SLURCH

SLARCH

SPLASH
?!

SLURCH
MÂCH
SCRUNCH
THE END

305

306

307

308

309

310

311

312

313

374

LP: 7
VIGILANCE: 1
BLOODY FISTS: 2 DQ
VICTORY ->295

282

69

242

102

157

315

IF YOU HAVE ALREADY BEEN IN IN THE CINEMA DURING YOUR ADVENTURE, YOU CAN NO LONGER GO TO 217.

316

317

BRRRR

RUN LIKE HELL TO 315!

318

155

AIIUUU
SPLASH

NICE SHOT! YOU DID IT IN ONE.

IT'S YOUR TURN TO KEEP WATCH. DO WHAT I DO, TRY NOT TO WASTE ARROWS.

I HOPE YOU'LL HAVE SOMETHING TO PRACTICE ON.

THERE ARE FEWER AND FEWER TARGETS.
THE END

320

NOW YOU JUST NEED TO FIND THE LOCK THAT GOES WITH THIS KEY. BY THE WAY, YOU CAN ONLY USE IT IF YOU HAVE 5 IP AT THE TIME (TAKE NOTE OF THIS). GO BACK TO 301.

321

NEVER TURN DOWN A FREE MEAL! HELP YOURSELF! WHEN YOU ARE DONE, GO BACK TO 3.

322

PUTTING ON THE UNIFORM ALLOWS YOU TO TAKE OFF 1 DQ FROM ALL ENEMY BLOWS AND GAIN 1 SP. PUTTING ON THE UNIFORM ALLOWS YOU TO TAKE OFF 1 DQ FROM ALL ENEMY BLOWS.

GO TO 298.

323

YIPEE! THIS FUN LITTLE BREAK GETS YOU 1 LP.

324

I325

IF YOU DON'T KNOW IT, GO BACK TO 300.

R326

327

328

T329

330

331

332

333

334

335

336

337

338

339

340

341

342

343

344

345

O346

347

348

NOW THAT'S SERIOUS INDIGESTION! YOU EMPTY YOUR STOMACH OF 500 OZ OF FLESH (OF YOUR CHOICE) AND LOSE 5 LP. GO BACK TO 242.

349

THE FENDER BENDER MAKES YOU LOSE 7 LP. GO BACK TO 250... IF YOU ARE STILL ALIVE.

350

IF YOU HAVE A SOLDIER'S UNIFORM AND AT LEAST 5 IP GO TO 119. OTHERWISE, GO TO 12.

I/A351

YOU CAN'T POSSIBLY TAKE BOTH OF THEM WITH YOU IN YOUR GROUP, SO YOU HAVE TO MAKE A CHOICE. ONCE YOU HAVE DONE THAT, GO BACK TO WHERE YOU CAME FROM (I OR A).

352

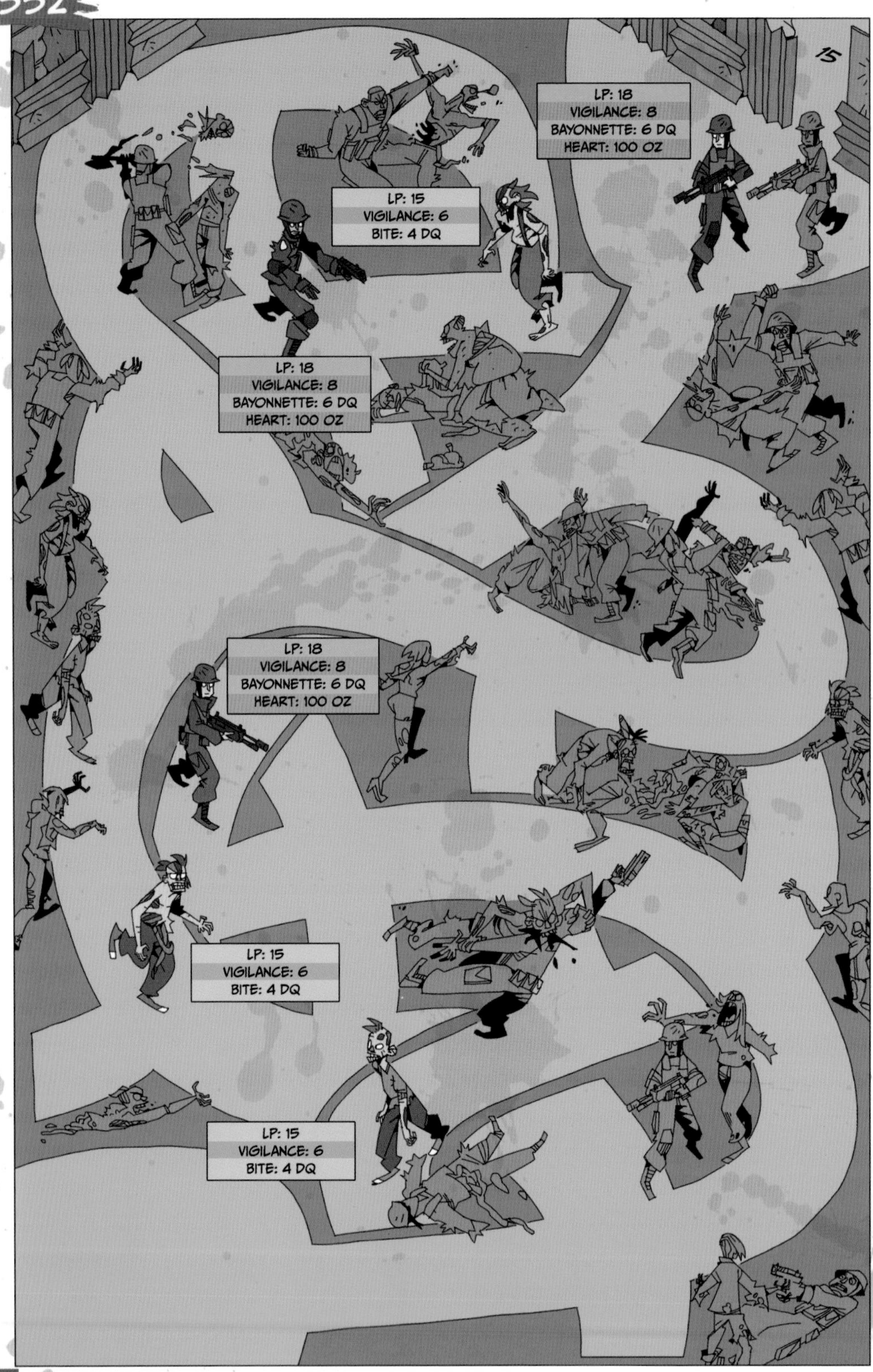

15
LP: 18
VIGILANCE: 8
BAYONNETTE: 6 DQ
HEART: 100 OZ
LP: 15
VIGILANCE: 6
BITE: 4 DQ
LP: 18
VIGILANCE: 8
BAYONNETTE: 6 DQ
HEART: 100 OZ
LP: 18
VIGILANCE: 8
BAYONNETTE: 6 DQ
HEART: 100 OZ
LP: 15
VIGILANCE: 6
BITE: 4 DQ
LP: 15
VIGILANCE: 6
BITE: 4 DQ

353

LP: 7
VIGILANCE: 3
BITE: 3 DQ

284

195

354

181

332

355

356

357

358

HEART: 300 OZ
BRAIN: 100 OZ
MUSCLE: 200 OZ

61

152

359

360

361

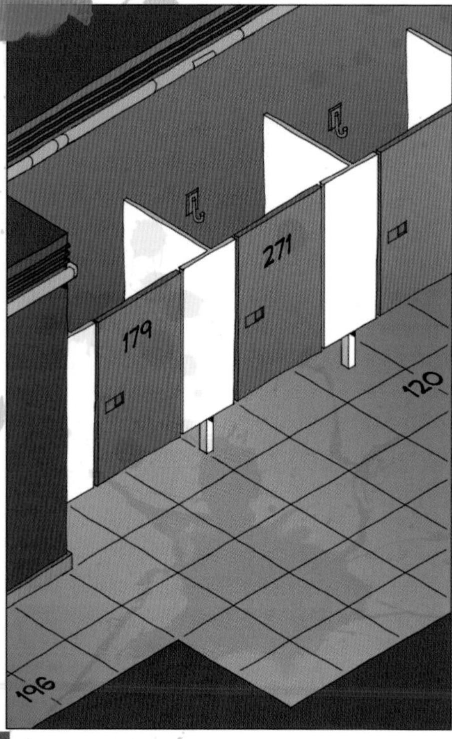

362

363

364

365

366

367

368

369

370

371

372

373

374

375

376

377

378

379

AND HERE'S ONE YOU WON'T HAVE TO FIGHT... CONTINUE ON TO 32.

K/V/Y380

YOU CAN'T TAKE THAT STINKING BEAST WITH YOU... GO BACK TO WHERE YOU CAME FROM (PANEL Y, V, OR K).

381

NOW THAT'S SERIOUS INDIGESTION! YOU LOSE 5 LP. GO BACK TO 261.

W382

WILSON'S BS CANCELS OUT XIAO'S SKILLS... TAKE NOTE AND GO BACK TO 282 (UNLESS IF YOU CAN GO TO K97 OR T35).

383

384

LP: 12
VIGILANCE: 12
WEAPON: GUN (7 DQ, 2 AM, 5 IP)
HEART: 100 OZ
BRAIN: 200 OZ
MUSCLE: 100 OZ
VICTORY -> 80

ADD UP YOUR BONUS POINTS AND TAKE THE PATH INDICATED BELOW ACCORDING TO YOUR SCORE.
BETWEEN 1 AND 7 BONUS POINTS: YOU'RE A LONER, GO TO 122.
BETWEEN 8 AND 15 POINTS: YOU'RE A PROTECTOR, GO TO 259.
OVER 15 BONUS POINTS: YOU'RE A HERO, GO TO 319.

ADD UP YOUR BONUS POINTS AND TAKE THE PATH INDICATED BELOW ACCORDING TO YOUR SCORE.

BETWEEN 0 AND 10 BONUS POINTS: YOU'RE A VEGETARIAN, GO TO 105.

BETWEEN 11 AND 20 BONUS POINTS: YOU'RE A CANNIBAL, GO TO 169.

OVER 20 BONUS POINTS: YOU'RE BULIMIC, GO TO 304.

A

ANDREA, THE NURSE	
BONUS POINTS: 3 SKILLS: FIRST AID. HER MEDICAL KNOWLEDGE ALLOWS YOU TO DOUBLE THE EFFECTS OF SURVIVAL OBJECTS. CHARACTER TRAIT: VOLUNTEER C274/I351 GO BACK TO 301.	BONUS POINTS: 3 LP: 15 VIGILANCE: 5 WEAPON: SCALPEL (4 DQ, 2 IP) HEART: 600 OZ BRAIN: 400 OZ MUSCLE: 100 OZ VICTORY -> 320 FLEE -> 301

B

BORIS, THE NUT CASE	
BONUS POINTS: 0 SKILLS: CRAZY! THIS GUY FLIPS OUT AND ATTACKS ANYTHING THAT MOVES... EVEN YOU! LP: 15 WEAPON: IRON BAR (5 DQ) YOU CAN FLEE TO 79 BUT YOU LOSE 1 SP. VICTORY -> 276	BONUS POINTS: 1 LP: 15 VIGILANCE: 8 WEAPON: IRON BAR (5 DQ, 3 IP) HEART: 300 OZ BRAIN: 50 OZ MUSCLE: 300 OZ VICTORY -> 79 FLEE -> 79

C

CAMILLE, THE PREGNANT WOMAN	
BONUS POINTS: 5 SKILLS: BIG BELLY. HER STATE MAKES GETTING AROUND DIFFICULT, THEREFORE EVERY TIME YOU ENCOUNTER AN ENEMY YOU HAVE TO ADD 1 VIGILANCE POINT PER ZOMBIE OR REMOVE 1 SURVIVAL OBJECT FROM YOUR BAG. CHARACTER TRAIT: MATERNAL A130/Q85/285 GO BACK TO 16.	BONUS POINTS: 5 LP: 15 VIGILANCE: 5 WEAPON: KNIFE (4 DQ, 2 IP) HEART: 600 OZ BRAIN: 500 OZ MUSCLE: 100 OZ VICTORY -> 345 FLEE -> 16

D

DENISE, THE DRIVER	
TO GET ON THE MINIBUS, GO TO 136. OR GO BACK TO 250.	TO ATTACK THIS CHARACTER, GO TO 349. OR GO BACK TO 250.

E

EDDY, PARANOID
LP: 15
VIGILANCE: 2
WEAPON:
SHOTGUN (9 DQ, 2 AM)
VICTORY -> 103
FLEE -> 149
BONUS POINTS: 3
LP: 15
VIGILANCE: 2
WEAPON: SHOTGUN
(9 DQ, 2 AM, 7 IP)
HEART: 900 OZ
BRAIN: 400 OZ
MUSCLE: 500 OZ
VICTORY -> 103
FLEE -> 149

F

WHOA, WAIT! I'M SURE WE CAN DO SOME BUSINESS TOGETHER...
IF YOU HAVE AT LEAST 5 IP, GO TO 347.
FRANK, THE HOODLUM
FRANK WON'T GO WITH YOU BUT HE'LL DO SOME DEALS WITH YOU.
TO GIVE HIM 1 SURVIVAL OBJECT, GO TO 288.
TO GIVE HIM 3 OR ONE FIRST AID KIT, GO TO 327.
TO GIVE HIM A WEAPON (MINIMUM 3 DQ), GO TO 193.
BONUS POINTS: 2
LP: 14
VIGILANCE: 2
WEAPON: CROWBAR
(6 DQ, 4 IP)
HEART: 400 OZ
BRAIN: 400 OZ
MUSCLE: 300 OZ
VICTORY -> 268
FLEE -> 55

G

GUY, THE PSYCHOPATH
BONUS POINTS: 1
SKILLS:
VIOLENT. THIS MAN WILL NOT SHUT UP FOR ANYTHING. HIS ABILITY TO ELIMINATE HIS ENEMIES IS IMPRESSIVE AND GIVES YOU 2 DQ PER BLOW AS LONG AS HE IS WITH YOU.
CHARACTER TRAIT: WORRYING.
GO TO 273.
BONUS POINTS: 1
LP: 22
VIGILANCE: 7
WEAPON:
WILD FISTS (6 DQ)
HEART: 100 OZ
BRAIN: 100 OZ
MUSCLE: 100 OZ
VICTORY -> 98
FLEE -> 182

H

HECTOR, THE NERVOUS NELLY
TO CHARGE RIGHT IN, GO TO 68.
TO GET HIM TO JUMP SO YOU CAN HELP HIM, GO TO 111.
TO TRY AND GET THIS EASY PREY, GO TO 306.
IF YOU HAVE A KNIFE AND AT LEAST 5 IP GO TO 331. OTHERWISE, LET THE OTHER ZOMBIES TAKE CARE OF HIM AND GET ON YOUR WAY THROUGH 212.

I

IVAN, THE GEEK	
BONUS POINTS: 2 SKILLS: GAMER. HIS KNOWLEDGE OF ZOMBIES ALLOWS YOU TO AVOID ALL COMBAT IN EXCHANGE FOR A SURVIVAL OBJECT. CHARACTER TRAIT: SURVIVOR A351 GO TO 51.	BONUS POINTS: 2 LP: 12 VIGILANCE: 3 WEAPON: BROAD SWORD (4 DQ, 3 IP) HEART: 200 OZ BRAIN: 600 OZ MUSCLE: 100 OZ VICTORY -> 278 FLEE -> 107

J

JOHNNY, THE BIKER	
JOHNNY WON'T COME WITH YOU, BUT TO THANK YOU FOR YOUR HELP, HE CAN DO YOU A FAVOR. TO LEARN ABOUT THE BEST WAY TO PROTECT YOURSELF AGAINST ZOMBIES, GO TO 296. TO LEARN THE BEST WAY TO GET RID OF A ZOMBIE, GO TO 342. TO TALK TO HIM ABOUT HIS BIKE, GO TO 240. (IF YOU HAVE AT LEAST 1 BONUS POINT).	BONUS POINTS: 2 LP: 18 VIGILANCE: 4 WEAPON: CROW BAR (6 DQ, 4 IP) HEART: 400 OZ BRAIN: 200 OZ MUSCLE: 600 OZ VICTORY -> 287 FLEE -> 265

K

KARIM, THE JOCK	
BONUS POINTS: 2 SKILLS: BRUTE FORCE. YOU CAN COUNT ON HIS HELP DURING YOUR FIGHTS. AS LONG AS HE IS WITH YOU, YOU GET AN EXTRA DQ PER BLOW. CHARACTER TRAIT: A TOUGH GUY. V380/Y380/X97/T329 GO BACK TO 170.	BONUS POINTS: 2 LP: 18 VIGILANCE: 8 WEAPON: IRON BAR (5 DQ, 3 IP) HEART: 600 OZ BRAIN: 200 OZ MUSCLE: 1 LB VICTORY -> 170 FLEE -> 170

L

LAMBERT, THE HANDIMAN	
BONUS POINTS: 0 THIS GUY WILL NOT HELP YOU UNTIL HE'S FOUND HIS DAUGHTER ZOE (239). GO BACK TO 172.	BONUS POINTS: 2 LP: 22 VIGILANCE: 7 WEAPON: AX (6 DQ, 4 IP) HEART: 600 OZ BRAIN: 500 OZ MUSCLE: 300 OZ VICTORY -> 188 FLEE -> 172

M

MICHAEL, THE RED FISH	
BONUS POINTS: 1 SKILLS: DECORATION. THIS RED FISH IS VERY PRETTY, BUT WILL BE OF NO HELP TO YOU WHATSO-EVER IN YOUR ESCAPE. CHARACTER TRAIT: QUIET. GO BACK TO 4.	BONUS POINT: 1 LP: 3 VIGILANCE: 0 WEAPON: FIN (1 DQ) HEART: 50 OZ BRAIN: 50 OZ MUSCLE: 50 OZ VICTORY -> 277 FLEE -> 4

N

NORBERT, THE COP	
BONUS POINTS: 2 SKILLS: PROTECT AND SERVE. HIS JOB AS A POLICEMAN IS TO PROTECT YOU. HE CAN TAKE BLOWS FOR YOU, BUT BE AWARE THAT HE HAS ONLY 18 LP AND REFUSES TO USE THE SURVIVAL OBJECTS. CHARACTER TRAIT: PROTECTOR GO TO 267.	BONUS POINTS: 2 LP: 18 VIGILANCE: 7 WEAPON: GUN (7 DQ, 4 AM, 5 IP) HEART: 300 OZ BRAIN: 300 OZ MUSCLE: 300 OZ VICTORY -> 75

O

ODILE, THE WOUNDED WOMAN	
BONUS POINTS: 3 SKILLS: OPEN WOUNDS. THE SMELL OF HER INFECTED WOUNDS MAKE THE ZOMBIES MORE AGGRESSIVE AND AUGMENTS THEIR DAMAGE BY ONE POINT. CHARACTER TRAIT: BADLY INJURED A237 GO TO 131.	BONUS POINTS: 1 LP: 7 VIGILANCE: 1 WEAPON: AX (6 DQ, 4 IP) HEART: 300 OZ BRAIN: 300 OZ MUSCLE: 300 OZ VICTORY -> 333 FLEE -> 184

P

PATRICK, THE ZOMBIE (OR NOT)	
YOU CAN STILL RUN AWAY TO 367, BUT IT WOULD COST YOU 4 LP. LP: 12 WEAPON: KNIFE (4 DQ) VICTORY -> 175	BONUS POINTS: 1 LP: 12 VIGILANCE: 5 WEAPON: KNIFE (4 DQ, 2 IP) HEART: 300 OZ BRAIN: 50 OZ MUSCLE: 500 OZ VICTORY -> 290 FLEE -> 367

Q

QUENTIN, THE KID

BONUS POINTS: 5
SKILLS: BLAH BLAH BLAH. HIS GIFT OF GAB ATTRACTS ZOMBIES' ATTENTION. IN EVERY FIGHT THE ENEMY STRIKES FIRST.
CHARACTER TRAIT: CHATTY.
Z238/C85
GO BACK TO 73.

BONUS POINTS: 5
LP: 8
VIGILANCE: 5
WEAPON: KNIFE (4 DQ, 2 IP)
HEART: 600 OZ
BRAIN: 100 OZ
MUSCLE: 200 OZ
VICTORY -> 178
FLEE -> 73

R

ROBERT, THE WOUNDED MAN

BONUS POINTS: 3
SKILLS: OPEN WOUNDS. THE SMELL OF HIS INFECTED WOUNDS MAKE THE ZOMBIES MORE AGGRESSIVE AND AUGMENTS THEIR DAMAGE BY ONE POINT.
CHARACTER TRAIT: BADLY INJURED
A48
GO TO 340.

BONUS POINTS: 1
LP: 7
VIGILANCE: 3
WEAPON: GUN (7 DQ, 4 AM, 5 IP)
HEART: 300 OZ
BRAIN: 300 OZ
MUSCLE: 300 OZ
VICTORY -> 59
FLEE -> 204

S

ARMY SOLDIER

THIS MAN IS TOO BADLY INJURED TO BE TRANSPORTED. WHAT ARE YOU GOING TO DO?
I82
A146
IF YOU WANT TO BE WITH HIM DURING HIS SUFFERING, GO TO 113.
TO PUT HIM OUT OF HIS AGONY, GO TO 190.

BONUS POINTS: 2
LP: 10
VIGILANCE: 3
WEAPON: FIST (3 DQ)
HEART: 400 OZ
BRAIN: 400 OZ
MUSCLE: 400 OZ
VICTORY -> IF YOU HAVE MORE THAN 5 IP, GO TO 322. OTHERWISE, GO TO 298.
FLEE -> 92

T

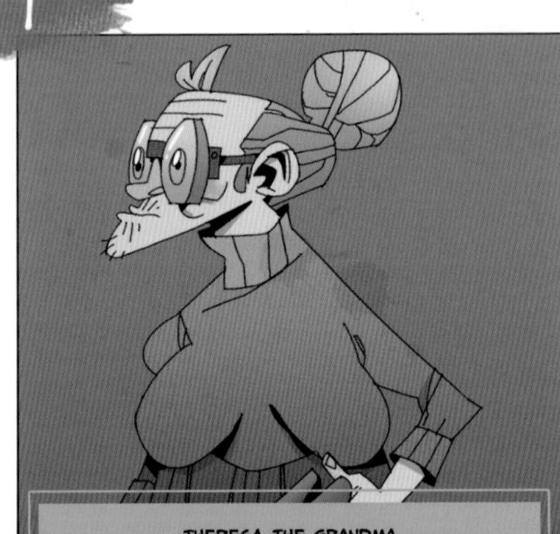

THERESA, THE GRANDMA

BONUS POINTS: 2
SKILLS: NOSTALGIC. VERY ATTACHED TO HER OLD GUN (8 DQ). YOU HAVE TO GIVE HER ONE SURVIVAL OBJECT EVERY TIME YOU WANT TO USE IT.
CHARACTER TRAIT: COMPLAINER
K176/X293
GO BACK TO 261.

BONUS POINTS: 2
LP: 12
VIGILANCE: 5
WEAPON: OLD GUN (8 DQ, 3 AM, 6 IP)
HEART: 200 OZ
BRAIN: 200 OZ
MUSCLE: 200 OZ
VICTORY -> 381
FLEE -> 265

U

ULYSEES, THE BUM

BONUS POINTS: 1
W14
TO WAKE UP THIS POOR GUY, GO TO 89.

BONUS POINTS: 1
THIS IS AN EASY NO FUSS MEAL! GET RIGHT TO IT WITHOUT HAVING TO FIGHT FOR IT!
HEART: 200 OZ
BRAIN: 200 OZ
MUSCLE: 200 OZ
WHEN YOU'RE FULL, GO TO 235.
IF YOU'RE NOT HUNGRY, GO TO 109.

V

VICK, THE DOG

BONUS POINTS: 2
SKILLS: SACRIFICES HIMSELF. THIS DOG CAN KILL ANY ENEMY FOR YOU BUT IT WILL COST HIM HIS LIFE (YOU HAVE TO TAKE HIM OUT OF YOUR GROUP AND YOU LOSE HIS BONUS POINTS).
CHARACTER TRAITS: LOYAL
K380
GO TO 247.

BONUS POINTS: 2
LP: 10
VIGILANCE: 7
WEAPON: JAWS (5 DQ)
HEART: 400 OZ
BRAIN: 100 OZ
MUSCLE: 500 OZ
VICTORY -> 247

W

WILSON, THE WRITER

BONUS POINTS: 3
SKILLS: SPACE CADET. IN THE EVENT OF A SURPRISE ATTACK HE WILL BE CAUGHT AND EATEN WITHOUT YOU BEING ABLE TO SAVE HIM... BUT YOU CAN AVOID THE FIGHT.
CHARACTER TRAIT: DISTRACTED
X86
GO BACK TO 155.

BONUS POINTS: 3
LP: 15
VIGILANCE: 3
WEAPON: PEN (2 DQ, 1 IP)
HEART: 300 OZ
BRAIN: 600 OZ
MUSCLE: 100 OZ
VICTORY -> 318
FLEE -> 91

X

XIAO, THE WAITRESS

BONUS POINTS: 2
SKILLS: FLEXIBLE. HER TALENT AND REFLEXES ALLOW YOU TO GET 1 LP IN A PANEL IN EXCHANGE FOR ONE SURVIVAL OBJECT.
CHARACTER TRAIT: FEMININE
K97/T35/W382
GO BACK TO 282.

BONUS POINTS: 2
LP: 15
VIGILANCE: 9
WEAPON: BASEBALL BAT (5 DQ, 3 IP)
HEART: 200 OZ
BRAIN: 200 OZ
MUSCLE: 600 OZ
VICTORY -> 313
FLEE -> 282

Y

YETI, THE HAMSTER

BONUS POINTS: 1	BONUS POINTS: 1
SKILLS: DECORATION. THE HAMSTER IS VERY CUTE, BUT WON'T HELP YOU AT ALL IN YOUR ESCAPE.	LP: 5
CHARACTER TRAIT:	VIGILANCE: 2
NERVOUS	WEAPON: TINY TEETH (1 DQ)
K380	HEART: 50 OZ
GO BACK TO 302.	BRAIN: 50 OZ
	MUSCLE: 50 OZ
	VICTORY -> 302
	FLEE -> 302

Z

@

Gogole

zombie weaknesses

zombie weaknesses	171 results
zombie invasion	260 results

g Lucky

More

IF YOU HAVE FEWER THAN 6 IP OR THIS DOESN'T INTEREST YOU, GO BACK TO 25.

€

JUDY'S ADVENTURE LOG SHEET

LP (Life points):

SP (Stealth points):

Bonus points:

Weapon 1	Weapon 2
Ammunition:	Ammunition:
Damage:	Damage:

quipment:	group: 1 SP = 1 ally
1	1
2	2
3	3
4	4
5	5
6	6
7	7
8	8
9	9
10	10

Notes:

Pick up at panel:

BEN'S ADVENTURE LOG SHEET

LP (Life points):

IP (Intelligence points):

Bonus points:

Weapon 1

Ammunition:

Damage:

IP:

Weapon 2

Ammunition:

Damage:

IP:

Equipment:

1

2

3

4

5

6

7

8

9

10

stomach:

heart

oz

brain

oz

muscle

oz

Notes:

Pick up at panel: